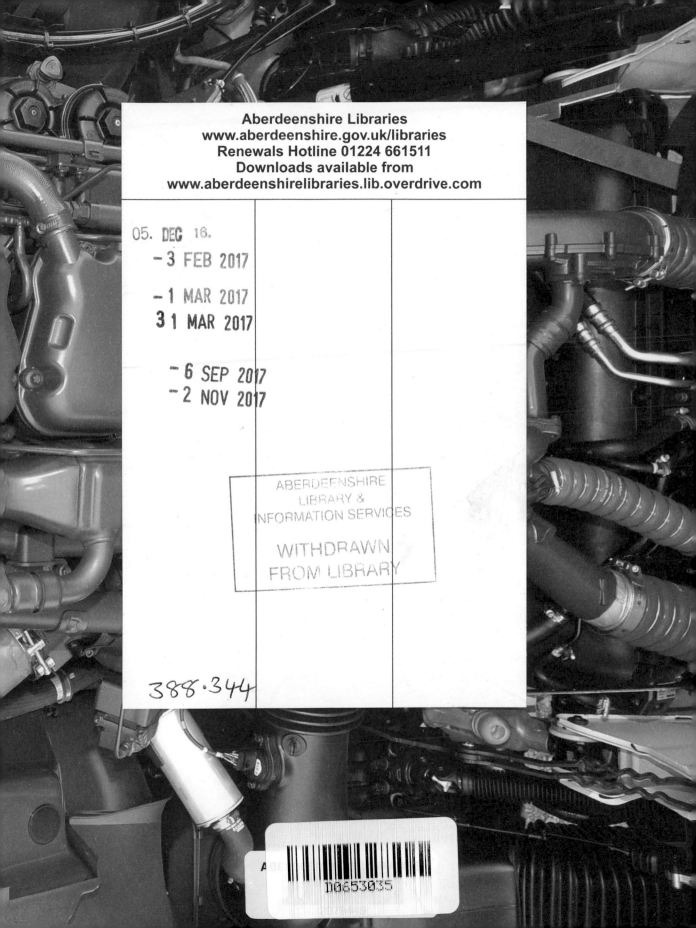

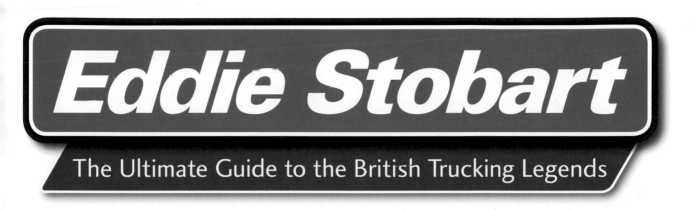

Eddie Stobart

The Ultimate Guide to the British Trucking Legends

Eddie Stobart

The Ultimate Guide to the British Trucking Legends

Martin Roach

Contents/

Introduction/

There have been three distinct phases in the remarkable history of Eddie Stobart. Firstly, Eddie Stobart himself set up an agricultural contracting business that established itself as a strong contender in the local marketplace around his home near Carlisle; secondly, his fiercely ambitious son Edward took over the reins in the 1970s and transformed this relatively small concern into a national haulage business that subsequently re-invented an industry; and thirdly, after a spate of undeniably dark days, Edward's brother William along with his childhood friend Andrew Tinkler grasped the opportunity to seize Stobart back from the brink and have since reignited a legend with a corporate comeback of stellar proportions.

Yet the history of Eddie Stobart is more than just the story of a hugely successful company. It is also about the people behind the famous name that is splashed down the side of thousands of lorries. The key personalities at the heart of the tale are stand-out entrepreneurs, colourful characters with a determination to succeed that has proven to be staggeringly powerful. Then there is the army of Stobart drivers and workers, proud to wear the famous uniform; and, of course, there are the Eddie Spotters, a legion of fans dedicated to following the famous red-and-green lorries. So this book was always going to be so much more than a company history; it will inevitably also encompass a series of fascinating biographies, personal vignettes and even an unusual take on celebrity, as well as, of course, the chronicle of an historically important haulage firm.

The view that Eddie Stobart has a massive, intangible 'X factor' was confirmed in 2010 by the filming of the television show *Eddie Stobart: Trucks & Trailers*, which proved so popular in the ratings that it turned a number of the company's drivers into celebrities and sent the firm's already mighty brand profile sky-high. A hit TV show about a haulage business? Improbable yes, but as I found out during my research, nothing seems beyond the Stobart empire.

When I was first asked to write a book about Britain's most famous haulage company, the (entirely selfish) question that instantly sprang to mind was, 'Can I drive one of their trucks?' Luckily, I was able to do exactly that and writing about that fabulous experience reinforced for me just how incredibly skilled these truck drivers are. There were many other questions vying for an answer when I started to research the project. For example, behind the TV documentary and high-profile drivers, how had this particular haulier managed to stand out from its commercial rivals so markedly? Why did those fans start to follow the brand? What was it about the Stobart family that had transformed a Cumbrian agricultural contractor into a business turning over more than half a billion pounds a year? In short, how had Eddie done it?

There were other more specific questions too: I wanted to go on a delivery to see what daily life was actually like for the thousands of Stobart drivers who travel up and down the road networks of Britain and parts of Europe. I wanted to delve into the numerous vehicles on the fleet, from the standard 'curtain-siders' (the workhorses of the company) to the specialist trucks that operate within niche industries such as logging and biomass. And I wanted to discover how two low points in the early 2000s and 2010 had been overcome so spectacularly by the current COO William Stobart and CEO Andrew Tinkler, who have subsequently turned their trucking firm into an ultra-modern multi-modal logistics company that is, in short, a phenomenon.

At the time of writing, Eddie Stobart makes a delivery every four-and-a-half seconds, and if you are driving on a motorway in the UK you will most likely see one of their famously liveried trucks every four-and-a-half minutes. The staggering scale of the firm's operation delivers sixteen million tonnes of goods on twenty-six million pallets every year. This is how Eddie Stobart does it.

Martin Roach

Part One/

The Eddie Stobart Story

This major development coincided with Eddie's 16-year-old son Edward taking a much more dominant role after he left school. Edward's final school report suggested that his academic achievements were only modest but that he was extremely good at repairing machinery. When Edward was 14, he had learned how to drive a JCB around the farmland, even though at the time this would have been illegal on public roads; after he left school he would often help his dad dig foundations or spread fertilizer, even at such a young age. He would always work around the yard with his much younger brother, William, beside him. They would both wash the wagons and machinery fanatically when all of the workers had gone home each night.

'It was a built-in driver's code,' William Stobart told the author. 'Whatever long day the driver had had, he would return to the farm and wash the truck, fill it up with fuel, clean the mirrors, irrespective of how late it was. Those drivers were the ones that taught us the importance of hygiene. Eventually I would wash trucks all weekend, every weekend.'

The year 1970 also saw the purchase of the haulage company's first articulated lorry, a Scania 110 Super (always called an 'artic', never a 'juggernaut', which any self-respecting trucker considers a pejorative term). This would be the start of an obsessive three decades of constant expansion of the fleet, spearheaded by Edward. Back then, when resources were so limited, William remembers the pure thrill of a new vehicle arriving: 'If we got a new truck, which was maybe only once or twice a year, it was the biggest highlight. For six months I'd be waiting for it to be coming. Me dad wasn't into the detail of paint jobs like me and Edward, so usually Stobart would be written slightly differently on each truck, there'd always be summat different because me dad didn't go into the detail and that used to really annoy me, even at such a young age!'

It wasn't just Edward that William spent time with. The youngest Stobart child's very first trip out in a truck came aged just nine. 'We had a driver called Norman

Early Beginnings

HOW A RURAL CUMBRIAN FAMILY BACKGROUND INSPIRED THE EDDIE STOBART LEGEND; FARM TRACTORS, HORSES, CHICKENS AND A CHILDHOOD SWEETHEART.

The contrast is stark: Eddie Stobart's proudly rural upbringing inspired a modest farm business, yet his name is emblazoned down the side of more than two thousand trucks owned by the most famous haulage firm in Britain. In 2011, the haulage company that Eddie started back in the 1960s turned over more than half a billion pounds, employing over 5,500 people in the process, with haulage, rail, port and air divisions operating deep into Europe. How that happened is a triumph of British ingenuity stretching across four decades, played out by a father and then in turn his two sons, all with an undying work ethic, an obsessive eye for detail and a determination and fierce passion to succeed.

Early Beginnings

How a rural Cumbrian family background inspired the Eddie Stobart legend; farm tractors, horses, chickens and a childhood sweetheart.

The contrast is stark: Eddie Stobart's proudly rural upbringing inspired a modest farm business, yet his name is emblazoned down the side of more than two thousand trucks owned by the most famous haulage firm in Britain. In 2011, the haulage company that Eddie started back in the 1960s turned over more than half a billion pounds, employing over 5,500 people in the process, with haulage, rail, port and air divisions operating deep into Europe. How that happened is a triumph of British ingenuity stretching across four decades, played out by a father and then in turn his two sons, all with an undying work ethic, an obsessive eye for detail and a determination and fierce passion to succeed.

The start of this long-distance journey is the Cumbrian hills, set in a breathtakingly picturesque county that sits on the northwestern tip of England, teetering on the Scottish border. Among Cumbria's highlights are the Lake District, stunning mountains, such as Scafell Pike and Skiddaw, and hills, known as fells. Although modern Cumbria is home to numerous corporate giants such as *Nestlé*, *GlaxoSmithKline* and *Pirelli* and also hosts a thriving tourist industry, at the start of the twentieth century it was almost exclusively a rural economy. Scattered among the undulating countryside were hundreds of farms, where native Cumbrians worked the steep land as they had done for generations. And it was at one of these unassuming farms, nestled in the hills, that Eddie Stobart began a family firm that would go on to start a revolution.

The tiny village of Hesket Newmarket doesn't look like the epicentre of a revolution. With a tradition of almost entirely rural life, the village is little more than a hamlet, with a small strip of brick houses and a village green, as well as a pub (the last one of five, The Old Crown, became famous in 1999 for being saved by the community, thus becoming Britain's first fully co-operative pub). Taking the first part of its name from Nordic and Old English words for 'ash tree' and 'head' or 'hill', Hesket Newmarket remains reassuringly quaint to this day. William Wordsworth stayed in the village in 1803 and half a century later so too did Charles Dickens; the mountaineer Sir Chris Bonington also lived there for a while. Bonington's interest in the area is obvious: nearby is the larger village of Caldbeck, but travel a little further and the Skiddaw mountain on the northern edge of the Lakeland Fells is also close. The famous Lake Windermere is just thirty miles away; ten miles closer is Carlisle, the county town, the key centre of this very expansive but relatively isolated county.

Although there was a history of mining in the area – a redundant bygone industry hinted at by the various old signs and several remaining derelict sites scattered among the fells – the predominant employer in the early twentieth

century was agriculture. These so-called 'fell villages', clinging to the slopes of this elevated and beautiful county, were littered with busy, usually family-run farms. And it is from this local farming stock that the Stobart family comes.

In 1929, the year of the Great Depression in America and global economic stagnation, Eddie Stobart was born to parents Addie and John, followed

Above: *Stobart's spiritual origins: Hesket Newmarket.*

by his younger brother Ronnie. The Stobart family life was typical of the local farming populace; although Hesket Newmarket may have been centred around the elongated village green, in fact much of the community lay strewn in farms in the surrounding hills. It was exactly one such smallholding, perched on the top of a hill a short drive from Hesket Newmarket, where Eddie Stobart was born and bred.

The young Eddie was an ordinary performer at school and preferred to spend most of his free time helping out on the family farm or at church. His father was a lay preacher and his family life was staunchly religious. Eddie was never a scholar, a trait his sons would also share, but just like their father this disinclination towards academia would not hold them back.

Eddie would till the land, milk the cows (before and after school), collect eggs and generally live the life of a local farmer from a very young age. He enjoyed respite from the hard farm work when his dad took him out on a motorbike, at first sitting perched on the petrol tank, then later as a pillion passenger.

Sadly, aged just twelve, the young Eddie's life was turned on its head when his beloved mother died after a long illness. She was not yet even middle-aged and left behind a husband and two young boys; farm life was about to get much tougher. Later in his teens a cherished cousin whom Eddie adored would also die prematurely, aged just nineteen, yet another body blow for the young Cumbrian lad.

With Britain embroiled in the Second World War, boys across the nation were allowed time off school to help work the land, so despite his grief Eddie still had work to do. Family life would eventually begin to return to some semblance of normality when his father remarried and his new stepmother, Ruth Crame, was very warm and loving to her new stepsons Ronnie and fourteen-year-old Eddie. She and John would go on to have six further children.

It was around this time that Eddie first showed the streak of entrepreneurial spirit that would later help him set up his famous haulage firm (an instinct that would be passed on to his sons Edward and William). As a young lad working the fields and spending all his free time on the farm, Eddie had noticed there were dozens of rabbit burrows peppering the ground. Cleverly figuring out that wartime Britain needed as much food as possible, he set about collecting traps and snares and began capturing, then selling, the game at Carlisle market. When word of his activities spread, nearby farmers started asking Eddie to help rid their own fields of rabbits too. 'Eddie the Rabbit Catcher' was soon a very popular young lad to visit on market day. His school work didn't benefit from his burgeoning little business, of course, and by his own admission he wasn't at school all that regularly after the age of twelve, so keen was he to help bring in extra money at home. Around this time he also bought and sold a horse for a small profit and reinvested the money in a number of chicken sheds, again with an eye on how much mark-up he could make.

While the teenage Eddie was already proving to have business acumen, his father secured a contract with the local council for 'the services of a horse and cart man'. The guaranteed income was precious for the family, but it was young Eddie, rather than his father, who would actually be delivering the service! Eddie had previously bought an 'unbroken' horse and trained it himself to pull carts and

Top left: *Edward, Anne, William, John and the family dog, Tiny, 1963.*
Top right: *Eddie Stobart enjoys a rare day off.*
Middle left: *Eddie and Nora in the late 1950s with the John, Anne and William.*
Middle right: *William.*
Bottom left: *Edward, Anne and John.*
Bottom right: *The family, late 1968.*

Above: *The Stobart's farmyard was increasingly overwhelmed by warehouses and storage facilities.*

farm-machines, so he was more than capable of being the 'man' with the cart. According to one source, the day rate for the horse and cart was 27 shillings and sixpence.

With the war over but ration-book Britain still reeling from the six-year shock, the ambitious young Eddie Stobart passed his driving test aged 17, and immediately started ferrying his family around the local area, whilst also revealing an innate obsession with keeping his father's cars invariably spotlessly clean.

He also heard about an attractive young woman who lived in a village two miles away: she was also deeply religious and held in high regard by the local community. Despite this girl's difficult childhood – orphaned at four and brought up in a variety of foster homes – Nora Boyd was widely regarded as a gentle and kind soul. In a chivalrous gesture, having never met Nora, Eddie wrote her a letter in which he talked of his love for Jesus and God and also bravely suggested that they might at some point meet up. They did indeed meet in December 1946 and within five years, on Boxing Day 1951, they were married. At the time of writing, they have been married for 60 years.

Just before Eddie had met Nora, he'd sold his hen-houses (to his supportive father) and purchased a tractor and threshing machine from a veteran thresher, along with a list of two hundred supposedly 'reliable' customers. Unfortunately, the following months proved very hard as more than half of those customers chose not to use Eddie's new venture, wary of his young age. Undeterred, however, Eddie grafted away and gradually established his own reputation for honest, hard work of quality, notably always using immaculately clean machines. 'Always leave the stackyard tidy' was his simple tenet. Within three years he had to buy two more threshing machines to cope with demand; this was in addition to all the work he had to do with his father and brother around the farm.

After Nora and Eddie had married, they'd moved into a rather spartan farmhouse in Wigton, a neighbouring village of similarly modest repute to Hesket Newmarket, whose more recent famous residents have included broadcasters Melvyn Bragg and Anna Ford. Nora and Eddie were renting the property and felt very much at home but after their first-born Anne arrived the following year, soon followed by a second child, John, they realised they needed to move again to accommodate their growing family. Rather than continue renting, they bought a bungalow called Newlands Hill, which cost them £450 in 1953.

Eddie was now in his mid-twenties and on 21 November 1954 his third child was born at home, another boy, called Edward (never Eddie, so as to differentiate him from his father). This was the boy who would go on to revolutionise his father's haulage business. Around this time Eddie himself was beginning to crave his own business, separate from the threshing and farm stock company he was involved in with his brother and father. He'd noticed that the arrival of new technology in the form of the combine harvester had led to a decline in threshing work, but he also cleverly realised that this had in turn created a demand for machines that could spread so-called 'slag' on the fields as fertilizer.

In 1957 Eddie officially opened his own business for trading, under the name E. P. Stobart. His instinct for a niche would quickly prove correct and his new venture was soon overloaded with work. By the end of the second year of trading, the firm had nearly doubled its turnover.

With three children to feed and working long hours, Eddie's life was hectic and gruelling at times but he was never happier than when he was putting food on his family's table by virtue of hard graft – a righteous and Christian value that was an absolute central moral in his life. Talking to Noel Davidson for the 1998 book *Only The Best Will Do – The Eddie Stobart Story*, the head of the family still played down his profile, saying he wanted his biography to be 'a book which gives glory to God, and not Eddie Stobart. For I am nobody you know. Just a farmer's lad, whom God has blessed.'

STAT//

IN 2012 THE TRAILER FLEET CONTAINED 3,000 TRAILERS, MOSTLY TRADITIONAL CURTAIN-SIDERS, BUT ALSO INCLUDING 500 CHILLED REFRIGERATED UNITS AND 80 ROAD TRAINS FOR TINS AND CANS.

Left: *William's photograph of his father's first articulated truck, a Scania 110 Super, taken in 1970 in Hesket Newmarket, and (below) forty years later, a Scania R440 is caught on camera in the same spot.*

This quote is indicative of the single most important factor in Eddie Stobart's life: his faith. Seeing his own father work as a Methodist lay preacher was deeply influential on him, and so from a young age Eddie gave himself to God, attending church services frequently and with great vigour. He made no secret of the fact that Nora's own recent conversion to God had been a hugely attractive trait when they first met. As a couple, they were very well-known faces within the local Methodist community.

Back on the farm, there was a problem with the growing business, though: at first local farmers' merchants had delivered the slag to each farm and Eddie would turn up and spread the fertilizer with his machine. However, as business boomed, he wasn't always able to get slag delivered on site and he realised that, in order for his new company to expand, he needed one vital piece of equipment: a lorry. So in 1960 Eddie Stobart bought his first lorry, a four-wheeler Guy Invincible truck. With his instinctive need for cleanliness in all his business activities, Eddie arranged for his new lorry to be repainted, choosing the distinctive colour combination of Post Office red and Brunswick green. On each of the two doors, the signwriter's brush painted the legend: 'E. P. Stobart, Caldbeck 206, Cumberland'.

Although Eddie was very proud of his new lorry, in his eyes it was just a tool to use at work; he would not spend long nights poring over the bodywork or engine (as his two sons Edward and William later would). Unfortunately the Guy truck proved to be rather unreliable and a few months later it was traded in for a Ford Thames.

The firm E. P. Stobart soon became a force to be reckoned with in the local agricultural contracting business. After some initial problems when key clients went out of business, Eddie proved remarkably resilient and also flexible, shifting his business to meet an ever-evolving demand, leading to a second Ford Thames soon being acquired. It was at this point that the firm's name E. P. Stobart was altered to just Eddie Stobart on the livery. Demand became so great that even

//STAT

IF ALL THE TRUCKS IN THE
2012 STOBART FLEET WERE
PARKED END TO END, THEY
WOULD FORM A CONVOY MORE
THAN TWENTY MILES LONG.

Nora found herself behind the wheel of a Ford van at times, to help out. And it wasn't just at work that there were new demands: in November 1961, while the Stobarts were living in a caravan because their bungalow was being extended, the family was completed by the arrival of a fourth child, William.

The farmhouse was right in the middle of the farmyard, but as the business grew a sprawling estate began to encroach out towards the fields. The family were so busy with the firm at this point that Nora often put the new baby's carry-cot in the van with her on deliveries. Around this time, Eddie secured a lucrative deal to work with a slag supplier that was searching for convenient and affordable storage facilities for its product; this led to an enormous slag store being built at Newlands Hill. Soon, the huge store was like a beehive, surrounded by ever-growing numbers of Stobart lorries, busily supplying the local agricultural trade with slag. The family team had also started to realise that periodically farmers had overstocks of grain, hay and straw that might be sought after somewhere else in the local area, so collections and deliveries of these surplus goods also began to evolve. The 1960s would prove to be a decade of growing demand and very long working hours for Eddie and his wife.

Like his father, Edward Stobart was not a high flyer at school. All the Stobart children would attend the village's Howbeck school for the first eleven years of their lives, just a short distance from the green. For the Stobarts, however, it was a one-and-a-half mile walk from their elevated smallholding to the daily lessons. There were just two classes across all age groups, the epitome of a rural school. The eldest child Anne was naturally chatty and sociable and so fitted in well, whereas Edward was far more reserved, often sensitive and usually quiet. He was reasonable with numbers but hopeless with reading and writing.

When Edward reached the age of 11, he sat the entrance exams for a place at the coveted local grammar school but found the paper so difficult that he was unable to answer a single question – instead he simply drew pictures of tractors.

His failure that day led to him being sent to the lesser alternative of the secondary modern, Caldew School, Dalston, in 1965.

The fact that Edward was not naturally gifted at school was a constant struggle; worse still, he had a pronounced stutter. When Edward had been just seven, he'd climbed onto the roof of an outhouse to look at some repairs he'd overheard someone talking about, but he slipped and fell off; the shock brought on a stutter that very night. His father Eddie had also suffered from a stutter that had started aged ten when he'd smashed his thumb in a door (strangely, his stutter just dissipated in his late teens).

Above: *Edward (left), scribbling hard at Howbeck Primary School in Hesket.*

Edward did not particularly enjoy secondary school: he was not a natural socialiser and his academic struggles exacerbated this sense of isolation. Edward later told his biographer Hunter Davies in *The Eddie Stobart Story* that he did not establish many friendships in class: 'I'm not sure what [the other children] thought of me. A bit strange perhaps, eccentric. I was a bit of a loner – I never wanted to be in anyone's gang and I didn't have a best friend.'

Edward would spend most of his play-time helping out the school gardener, trying – and failing – to get a ride on the sit-on lawn mower. He was fascinated with machines and working around the farm. Every morning he would work from dawn around the yard; then, after trudging reluctantly to school, he would complete his classes and run home each day, eager to work on the machines again, helping out in the yard and tinkering with the tractors and lorries.

He was obsessed by the whole environment and notably more confident here than at school. Each day he would also walk to his grandfather's smallholding nearby to collect the family some milk. He also persuaded his dad to buy old railway sleepers which he chopped up and sold as kindling to teachers at school. According to Edward, by the age of 14 he'd saved up £200 (a huge sum in those days) and carried this cash around in his pockets. Young Edward Stobart was never shy of work. //

From Fertilizer to Fantasy

As the Swinging 1960s give way to the 1970s, the family firm evolves rapidly from a single-vehicle dream into a still modest but vibrant red and green fleet that sets about re-inventing an industry.

The year 1970 was a watershed in the Stobart story. By now they had six vehicles and six drivers busily spreading lime slag around the farms in their area; Eddie was more interested in this original side of the business and less passionate about the ever-growing haulage work that his son Edward was so fascinated with. So Eddie Stobart Limited was incorporated as a company, designed to focus on the haulage potential his son was keen to capitalise on. Meanwhile, Eddie himself would continue to sell fertilizers and slag as his own separate sole-trading business.

This major development coincided with Eddie's 16-year-old son Edward taking a much more dominant role after he left school. Edward's final school report suggested that his academic achievements were only modest but that he was extremely good at repairing machinery. When Edward was 14, he had learned how to drive a JCB around the farmland, even though at the time this would have been illegal on public roads; after he left school he would often help his dad dig foundations or spread fertilizer, even at such a young age. He would always work around the yard with his much younger brother, William, beside him. They would both wash the wagons and machinery fanatically when all of the workers had gone home each night.

'It was a built-in driver's code,' William Stobart told the author. 'Whatever long day the driver had had, he would return to the farm and wash the truck, fill it up with fuel, clean the mirrors, irrespective of how late it was. Those drivers were the ones that taught us the importance of hygiene. Eventually I would wash trucks all weekend, every weekend.'

The year 1970 also saw the purchase of the haulage company's first articulated lorry, a Scania 110 Super (always called an 'artic', never a 'juggernaut', which any self-respecting trucker considers a pejorative term). This would be the start of an obsessive three decades of constant expansion of the fleet, spearheaded by Edward. Back then, when resources were so limited, William remembers the pure thrill of a new vehicle arriving: 'If we got a new truck, which was maybe only once or twice a year, it was the biggest highlight. For six months I'd be waiting for it to be coming. Me dad wasn't into the detail of paint jobs like me and Edward, so usually Stobart would be written slightly differently on each truck, there'd always be summat different because me dad didn't go into the detail and that used to really annoy me, even at such a young age!'

It wasn't just Edward that William spent time with. The youngest Stobart child's very first trip out in a truck came aged just nine. 'We had a driver called Norman

Bell,' William says, 'and another one called Norman Glendinin, who both used to take me out. The latter used to take me the most of anyone. He would stop at the house where I'd be sat on the wall and he'd say, "Do you want to come out, boy?" He'd ask me mam if I could and I'd go out with him in his truck for most of the day delivering fertilizer. I was only nine but I remember every single day to the smallest detail, they were fantastic days.'

The family haulage firm might not yet have been the huge empire it would later become, but business was booming and in 1972 Eddie chose to diversify even more and bought derelict premises in Wigton, which he converted into a farm suppliers. Despite having very little spare time as the head of a family of six (he was soon to be a grandfather!), a thriving haulage business and livestock too, Eddie still devoted himself to church as he was a proudly religious man, and both he and Nora had very strict rules about home life. They always took their children to Sunday school and church without fail. Eddie himself had made his own first speech at Sunday school when he was just four years old and both parents encouraged their children to follow their spiritual path. 'Me dad was always at church on a Sunday, you couldn't watch telly on a Sunday, and he wouldn't even work on a wagon on a Sunday at all. I was twelve before we got a TV because he didn't agree with it.' The Stobart family wasn't poorly off – they had a Morris Oxford car, for example, and several people working for them – but they weren't exactly rich.

Importantly, also in 1972 Edward reached 18 and was given a thousand shares in the family firm, just as his sister Anne had been when she'd reached that age. Interestingly, although Anne, William and Edward were all involved in the family business from a young age, the second eldest child John had no interest in joining

//STAT

EDDIE STOBART HAS
TRANSPORTED GOODS FOR THE
PRINCE OF WALES, MIRROR
GROUP NEWSPAPERS, TESCO,
COCA-COLA AND BRITVIC
AMONG OTHERS.

the firm, so aged 18 he took a cash alternative to his thousand shares and excitedly set up his own farming business instead.

By this point there were three strands to the family's business interests: the traditional fertilizer side of agricultural contracting (run by Eddie's sole-trading company); the Wigton farm shop (again run by Eddie, ably assisted by Anne); and the relatively new haulage side (Edward's passion). The triple combination was clearly working because in 1972 they made profits of over £17,000!

Even though he was seven years younger than his brother Edward, William was always working around the farm, eager to help out. Growing up surrounded as he was by tractors and farm machinery, it is perhaps not surprising what the youngest Stobart child was fascinated with: a different type of horse-power.

'Me first poster was a Ford tractor. And my whole ambition was to have a Ford tractor. We had Fords at the time, well, me brothers did. I always wanted a Ford 7000, so that was the poster. In the early days that's all I wanted to do. First it was tractors, then cars came and then trucks… but as a young kid it was all about tractors.

'I was mad on trucks too. I knew every engine type,' continues William. 'I could tell the sound of every engine. We lived on that farm up on top of the hill, and there was a windy road that came up to the house, and you could hear a wagon coming a good five to ten minutes before it actually arrived, because it was such a steep climb. I could sit on a wall and tell the engine and make and gearbox and everything. In them days, British trucks fitted different engines, so you bought the truck and then spec'd what engine you wanted and they were made by different manufacturers. You could tell by the sound of the engine what it was, then you'd guess what gearbox it had and you could kind of guess what make it was too.

'The best present I ever had was *The Observer Book of Trucks*. It had every truck in there, this little square book, and that was the best gift I ever, ever got. I remember they used to update it every year or so and I'd always get the new edition. Then I wrote off to all the manufacturers and said me dad was thinking of buying their trucks – which he wasn't! – and could they send me some literature and books? I remember waiting eagerly for the post and they'd send me all this sales literature on a truck. Rolls-Royce engines, Gardner engines and Cummins would all send us stuff. That was me bedroom basically then, the walls were just covered in posters of trucks. I got caught pinching badges off a truck once, which me brother Edward had to take back!'

William appears to have nothing but cherished memories of his childhood: 'I grew up watching all this evolve, seeing the lorries come and go, I loved it. I got a camera for Christmas when I was ten, and so with a lot of them early photographs you will see a little dog called Tim in the picture. I was always actually taking a picture of him but there'd invariably be a truck in the background, and that's the pictures you see today!'

Due to the large age gap, William's experiences of school were somewhat different from his brothers': 'I can remember my first day at school when I was five, me brothers were already at secondary school, so I had no one there with me. When Edward left school at 15, I was still only eight. I went up to a secondary school with a thousand kids, from a village school that'd had only a few dozen kids, that was quite daunting. I'd started school with a speech impediment, which obviously wasn't good either.' William found his own surname particularly tricky; interestingly, no one recalls any accident similar to Eddie's or Edward's that brought on William's stutter, but the youngest of the Stobart boys thinks he might have subconsciously been copying his older brother.

William took after his older brother Edward academically too. 'We weren't high achievers at school, no. In them days at school, there wasn't a big effort to push for you to learn and scholar better: if you didn't want to do it, nobody at school really pushed you. Just like Edward, I went into the 'Progress Class' (with Mrs Carlisle) so basically if you couldn't keep up with your own class then instead of going to

Above: *The Wigton farm shop was successful and increasingly enjoyable for Eddie. The Stobarts often sold their farm produce and advertised their agricultural business at local fairs such as the Cumberland show.*

The 1970s Fleet

Top, left to right: *Blue Fire Lady, AEC six-wheeler;*
Lynda, ERF; Blondie and Julie, DAF DKS.
Middle, left to right: *Seddon Atkinson 400; Fiat;*
Suzy DAF 2200; Atkinson Borderer.
Bottom, left to right: *Helen, Leyland Buffalo; Olivia,*
DAF 2200 eight-wheeler; Julia, Scania 111; Caldbeck
Ranger, DAF2200.

Above: *A restored Robson's truck. William and Edward were very impressed by the smart livery.*

normal lessons you went in the Progress Class. This class had all the hard lads from school in it, so they were all thick, but hard!'

William liked Mrs Carlisle and began to improve steadily. The fact that some of the tough kids in the Progress Class stood up for him when he was being bullied about his speech impediment also helped his confidence and general happiness at school. Although a spell working with a speech therapist failed to help his stutter much, William continued improving in school generally and after three years was moved back into a 'normal' class.

'I got into that circle of kids in the Progress Class and it kind of worked. I started to catch up with me reading and writing. At the age of eleven I hadn't learned a lot; then I was at the secondary for four years but I stuck with it and tried hard and eventually I left school with a bit of maths. I could add up, I couldn't spell that well but I could read a certain amount. I used to buy the *Sun* newspaper everyday to teach me to read!'

When asked about his teenage memories, William automatically talks about working on the farm with the trucks, rather than thoughts of school. His recollections of being a teenage boy helping out his older brother Edward are still vivid: 'Every night I came home from school I would help out. We used to get fertilizer from the ports and it was all palletised, and we used to empty the trucks of a night, all hand-ball on to your shoulder and then on to pallets. It was easier for me being on the ground than it was for Edward up on the wagon! Every night after school there'd be a couple of wagons, and even in the dark we'd start to unload them. I was doing it because I wanted to, I probably got pocket money at the time, but it was the family business, it was what you did. You didn't really have a choice.

'On a Sunday, Edward would drive me in a car to Carlisle just to look at the wagons, like Robson's Transport who had fish wagons coming down from Scotland. They would pick up from the fishing boat on Saturday nights and leave early

Sunday morning for all the fish markets in the south of England, so Carlisle was a big stop-off point full of truck cafes, where the drivers would get a meal. Me and Edward would just go and sit in these truck stops and look for them coming in, just sitting there, keeping ourselves to ourselves. The trucks were beautiful, the livery had brightly coloured flags and emblems and all these amazing paint jobs. It was all we used to talk about; Edward's whole dream was having vehicles like that – they had the best tackle, the best wagons, the smartest paint jobs, and his whole ambition was to have exactly that. Edward dragged me with him all the time, he'd say 'Come on, we will get stuck in, we'll have a fleet of wagons like that one day . . .'

When Edward turned 21 in 1975, he passed his HGV Class 1 licence and so immediately began driving trucks for the family firm; from here on, he and William would regularly go out on deliveries together. Many 'drops' were for official business but they also continued their cherished trips to the truck cafes and depots just to sit and stare at the vehicles, with Edward constantly thinking about his grandiose haulage dreams.

Back at Newlands, Edward took on any driving jobs that the other men didn't like the sound of – the more urgent the better. He enjoyed providing a prompt and flexible service and particularly loved meeting supposedly 'impossible' deadlines. He was also constantly teaching himself about the business, visiting local haulage firms to listen to advice or sometimes just watch them in operation. Pretty soon Edward was running the haulage business as if it was his own. By 1976, he had eight trucks and twelve employees.

In 1977 William left school and immediately started helping his father by driving tractors and spreading lime and slag. By the age of 18 he would progress to driving a concrete mixer, too. It was around this time that William met and befriended a local lad who was one year his junior and who would go on to become a crucial part of the future Stobart story: Andrew Tinkler. The boys' parents knew of each other through church and the two lads had met a few years earlier at

STAT//

UNUSUAL LOADS INCLUDE THE LIGHTS AT PICCADILLY CIRCUS AND THE TURF FOR CARDIFF'S MILLENNIUM STADIUM.

various services. One summer, Andrew spent a day in a truck with his brother-in-law and they bumped into William who was out spreading. The two chatted and thereafter became firm friends. When William had got his driving licence aged 17, he and Andrew would go out chatting to girls together; eventually, Andrew and William would marry two sisters (having previously dated two other pairs of sisters!). During these teenage years, the two pals were great company for each other; in time their close and intense friendship would prove to be the saviour of the business.

The haulage branch of the business had continued to expand at such a rate that it had quickly outgrown the Newlands Hill site. Although 22-year-old Edward had taken charge of running this side of the family business, the physical requirements of the lorries could not be met at the farm. There were simply too many lorries, men and deliveries. Another problem was that of location: the 20 miles they had to drive to pick up any load from Carlisle meant longer journey times and larger fuel bills, so Edward felt that a base much nearer the county town was far more desirable; for local Carlisle firms, surely having a haulier right on their doorstep would be more attractive?

So the Stobarts found a suitable yard in Greystone Road in the Kingstown area of the city, not far from the Carlisle United football ground. This move cemented the family's venture into haulage as an actual business rather than a useful sideline. The rent for the yard was intimidating but Edward was not concerned, and his vision for the potential of the haulage business remained undimmed.

Initially the new depot was fairly ill-equipped to deal with the constant demands of a busy haulage firm, but Edward was undeterred and voraciously scouted for new work. The complex logistics of this side of the business never appealed to his father Eddie, so who better to do that than the deeply ambitious and energetic Edward? He was a natural. Edward enjoyed helping out at the Wigton Farm Shop but was mostly obsessed with the haulage business. When he

Top left: *As his sons built up the haulage side of the firm, Eddie continued with fertilizer and slag delivery.*
Top right: *Cleanliness was an obsession for Edward.*
Middle left: *Bob 'Big Mac' McKinnel joined Stobart in 1979 and still works for the company.*
Middle right: *William climbing into an Atkinson Borderer.*
Bottom left: *William at the wheel of an Atkinson Borderer.*
Bottom right: *Neville Jackson, another long-standing staff member, joined the company in 1978.*

EACH SUPERMARKET TRAILER
CAN CARRY AROUND 40-45
RETAIL CAGES PACKED WITH
FOOD SUPPLIES.

wasn't at home taking phone calls and planning drops, he was out in the yard working on the lorries or driving them himself.

His dad Eddie much preferred the banter of the farmers' auctions, the rapport he had with the local rural personalities and the long but rewarding hours working on the farm. He also felt that his faith always had to take precedence over his career; young Edward was also religious and proudly so, but his determination and ambition were absolute. He had lofty ideas about how to take the haulage business forward, he wanted to organise the firm more precisely and he was constantly looking for an ever-increasing number of contracts. He was not quite as fascinated as William was with the trucks in the yard – they were increasingly seen as a means to an end. But make no mistake: Edward Stobart was a young man on a mission.

Edward's timing seemed fortunate too. For many years, a surplus of 'owner-drivers' had flooded the haulage market with cheap labour and often poor-quality vehicles, so it was an industry that operated on a tiny profit margin. Despite this, with nearly a million trucks on the roads in the early 1970s, competition was very fierce. In addition, there was strict legislation and licence rules that restricted which firms could do what type of work – prior to 1968, for example, Stobart were not allowed to do national drops. However a change in the legislation in that year meant Stobart could then travel anywhere with any cargo. This opened up a whole new world for Edward: the country was now his oyster and he was not about to miss the opportunity. He started working even harder.

While the haulage firm was expanding all the time, albeit still only with agricultural loads, the core of the family income remained the supply, spreading and storage of slag and lime. However, in a peculiar twist of fate, in the same month in 1976 that the family lost their biggest contract for slag supply, they also received a call from a local company called Metal Box, enquiring whether Stobart might be able to collect and then store thousands of empty drinks cans to help them out over the particularly busy Christmas period. Following this unexpected phone call, and after a long night converting a six-wheel Ford truck that was only suitable for carrying lime into a truck fit for soft drinks cans, the first Eddie Stobart Ltd lorry to pick up a load that wasn't specifically for the agricultural trade arrived at Metal Box, bang on time. Just as Edward had promised it would. It was only a temporary contract, but Metal Box would later return to play a pivotal part in the Eddie Stobart story.

Above: *Immaculate as usual: Katie, DAF 2800.*

Edward Stobart's exacting eye for detail was becoming widely known. His trucks were always spotlessly clean, the signwriting on Stobart lorries was a work of art and his customers contracted him knowing that their goods would be delivered on time, in perfect condition and for the right price. Then in 1976, Edward also made a decision that would later define the entire business: he started naming his trucks after women.

Other local firms such as Robsons and Suttons were far larger concerns than Stobart, but Edward was after their crown. He'd noticed that Robsons sometimes named their trucks, usually with the word 'Border'. So for example they had a Border Laddie and a Border Patrol in their fleet. Edward took this idea one step further and decided to start naming his trucks after women, using a female moniker to neatly fill in the gap between the radiator and windscreen. This being 1976 and Edward being a young lad, he had a particular soft spot for the supermodel Twiggy so that was the very first name he used. Twiggy was followed soon after by Tammy (Wynette) then Dolly (Parton), Suzi (Quatro) and Tina (Turner). A seed had been planted that would later fascinate a nation.

Within a few short years, Eddie Stobart Ltd was forced to expand again and again and again, to cope with the increasing demands of their haulage and storage

Above: *Dolly, DAF DKS, named after country-and-western singer Dolly Parton.*

business. In the late 1970s and 1980s there was an ever-expanding network of motorways zig-zagging across Britain, and so there had been a seismic shift in the potential for national haulage. Prior to this, Cumbria had been a very long drive from almost any part of England; now the M6, albeit the only motorway in the county, could mainline industry and commerce from the once relatively isolated area right into the heart of Britain. Stobart were at the forefront of this revolution in transportation. Ironically, when he was old enough and had started driving tipper trucks, Edward himself had worked on the construction of the M6 motorway that would later prove so important to his haulage firm's success.

Edward's father Eddie Stobart was now in his fifties and was becoming increasingly involved in Christian work, setting up various church groups and even a chapel, enthusiastically organising rallies, as well as helping the Gideons and the local YMCA. 'Edward was very ambitious, very,' recalls William. 'If it hadn't been for Edward, me dad would have been dead happy selling fertilizers to the farmers, he was content with that. But me brother Edward wanted to progress the haulage firm.'

As William highlights, Edward was absolutely steadfast in his passion for the haulage business and worked relentlessly long hours developing the customer base and modernising the fleet, constantly upgrading, evolving and honing the company. He had certainly found his niche. Despite his reputation for cleanliness with his trucks, Edward himself had long hair at this point, he smoked and drank a little, albeit only like most young men, was generally covered in oil from working on trucks and was usually exhausted from his tireless working life. So although he was as keen on girlfriends as any of his friends, he wasn't particularly successful with them, not because they weren't interested but simply because he was more interested in the business. He would regularly cancel a date if an urgent job came into the office late at night and his habit of always accepting work – even when he didn't have a truck or driver to hand – meant he had to reorganise his week constantly. Work came first. Edward later admitted that between 1976 and 1986 he was doing office work all day and sometimes driving four or five nights a week too. When he eventually got married in 1980 to Sylvia Turner, they went on honeymoon to Morecambe, but returned the next day and Edward went out on a delivery. (Edward and Sylvia would later adopt four children from the same family, three girls and a boy).

Aside from Edward's nuptials, 1980 was a hugely eventful year for the family, as they took out a massive loan to build a colossal warehouse facility at a new site on the Kingstown industrial estate in Carlisle. They sold the Newlands Hill site and the farm shop to help with funding and took a massive risk. When they erected the new warehouse, it was a 19-year-old William who skimmed the concrete floor at 4.30 each morning to make sure the project was ready on time.

The completion of this new warehouse was symbolic of Eddie finally passing the baton on to his son, and Stobart legend has it that when Edward and his father surveyed the new project's completion, Edward turned to his father and said, 'Thanks Dad, I can manage now.' //

Top: *Sue Ellen, DAF 2800, named after Sue Ellen Ewing from TV series* Dallas. **Bottom:** *Toyah, Iveco, after 1980s punk singer Toyah Wilcox.*

The Smartest Truckers in the World

HOW THE 1980S AND 1990S SAW THE FAMILY FIRM TRANSFORM INTO AN ICONIC NATIONAL BRAND.

When asked about his famously tireless ambition, Edward Stobart once said, 'I like to drive without brakes.' Unfortunately, around 1980–1982, while Edward's father was retreating from the haulage business, so too were customers, because Britain was in the grip of a severe economic recession. For all Edward's passion and enthusiasm, he was battling against miserable market conditions which meant competition was fierce and profits meagre. Short working weeks were commonplace and the future of the firm was constantly threatened. Edward faced up to this in the best way he knew – he increased his workload.

When Edward wasn't organising and managing the business, he was doing the actual weekend and night-time driving. He would frequently get back to the depot very late and sleep in the Portakabin office that he had erected. His triple obsessions were 'price, service and presentation'. The new warehouse space meant that big customers could now be offered storage facilities as well as haulage, which even in a recession was an enticing proposition. Edward became well known for the phrase, 'No problem'.

He had a reputation for being a firm but fair boss. He expected his drivers to clean their trucks after a day's work, regardless of how late they returned to the depot. He later admitted that if he went home knowing that a truck was dirty in the depot, he couldn't sleep properly. This meticulous, almost obsessive cleanliness even resulted in several drivers having to stay late one Christmas Eve to wash their trucks. The lessons from his dad's drivers back at Newlands Hill had clearly been heeded.

Edward's obsession wasn't just for the sake of cleanliness; he knew there was an implied professional pride in his trucks being spotless. He was also keen to progress from carrying the so-called 'dirty' loads – lime slag and coal for example – and move on to more prestigious loads such as foodstuffs. He also rightly foresaw that the growth of supermarkets and food retailers in the UK would lead to far bigger business than farm contractors could ever dream of. And all of this complex work was mostly kept in Edward's head; he rarely wrote anything down but he always knew what was going on.

To carry foodstuffs, Edward knew he would need flat-bed trailers that could take clean wooden pallets; so he went out and bought two new trucks designed for this purpose. This time, instead of just painting the firm's name on each truck's door, as was the tradition in haulage, he also had the heavy plastic sheet that covered the long sides of the trailer – known as the curtain – branded with the legend 'Eddie Stobart' too. As William Stobart explains, this was unusual at the time: 'There was no vinyl lettering back then, it was all signwriting by hand. We put 'Eddie Stobart' down the side of every trailer from then on, which was something that a lot of companies didn't do. It wasn't the cost of painting the curtains that put people off, but the negative impact the signwriting might have on the residual value, the second-hand value, because you couldn't get it off your curtain very easily.'

The business continued to grow apace and Edward's working hours remained prolific. Fortunately, help was at hand when William turned 21 in 1982 and was able to realise his life-long ambition to get his truck licence. 'When I was a kid, all I wanted to do was drive a tractor, spreading lime. I knew that I would want a car licence as soon as I was old enough, but as a young lad I was happy just thinking about spreading the fertilizer. However, my real ambition was always to drive trucks.

'I'd already done two years of tractors but when me brother moved to Carlisle I worked in the garage and the office, answering phones 'cos Edward was planning the drops, and he would tell me what to do and I would help plan it. I worked a lot in the garage workshops too, washing trailers and repairing trucks. I was a mechanic most of the time in that period, but I longed to be 21.

'I was sat in a truck at midnight on me 21st birthday, I'd put the 'L' plates on and I was waiting till the clock ticked past midnight. I passed me test six days after me birthday. I'd booked me test prior, that was the earliest I could get it; on the day I thought I'd failed but they passed me.' In fact William passed his tractor test, HGV Class 1 and car test all first time.

'So I drove back to the yard and me brother said, "Right do a run to Scotland! Straight away!" It was already two in the afternoon but off I went, I picked up a trailer of cans to go to Glasgow. It was just amazing! Obviously it was a bit scary because I was very green, but this was my dream job, it was all I'd ever wanted to do.' William's first truck was a Scania 112 intercooler, fleet number 12, in 1983.

The 1980s Fleet

Top: *Nena, Volvo F7; Jemma, DAF 2500;*
Lesley Anne, Scania 112; Lisa Marie, DAF 2800.
Middle: *Lynda Louise, Seddon Atkinson 301; Molly Mack,*
DAF 2800; Carol, Volvo F10; Trudy, DAF 2800.
Bottom: *Rossi, DAF 2800; Lucy, DAF 2500;*
Carol Anne, Scania 82.

Above: *William Stobart's first truck.*

'You were driving all over the country,' he continues, 'but there wasn't many timed deliveries like these days. We still always pushed on because it was our own business but it was very different to today. At times back then you'd drive until you physically couldn't drive anymore. The laws were far more lax and some drivers knew how to get round them. So back then it was usual to do very long shifts, everybody did in them days.'

However, after just two years of his 'dream job', William was asked by Edward to leave his trucking paradise behind and take over the office. He had helped out previously in the office on occasion, but never enjoyed it. So this new proposal was not a particularly tempting prospect, but Edward was not easily denied and he eventually confronted William, saying that unless his younger brother took the role of office manager, he would employ an outsider to do the job. William acquiesced but not before a number of very heated rows.

'That was a bit of a culture shock because I wanted control, there were a lot of arguments for a few months and then we sort of all settled down and afterwards it went well really.' Fortunately this time William was in charge of the traffic desk, where his core role was to plan the drivers' routes and days, and unlike the more mundane office work he loved it. It was almost a vicarious way for him to continue his trucking life without compromising the growing family business. Due to his long-standing involvement with truckers and also his own experience of driving since he was a teenager, William quickly proved to be a complete natural. This was despite the fact that this graduate of the 'Progress Class' would still not have considered himself to be an accomplished writer. Instead, he developed his own set of phonetics in the office that were very simple for everyone around him to understand and use.

By 1984, Edward Stobart had 28 trucks and business was booming. From 1980 to 1985, the firm's turnover doubled to £1 million. By 1985 they had quadrupled the size of the firm since 1976, with 26 lorries, 32 trailers and 40 staff. Until now,

Edward, William and their drivers were still washing all these vehicles by hand but the time had come to finally acknowledge that they could no longer do this. Reluctantly, the brothers had to invest in an automated washing machine for the lorries, a state-of-the-art Karcher that cost £22,000.

At the same time, they made a joint decision to go for expansion, to recruit experts in the field and really make Eddie Stobart Ltd a force to be reckoned with, on a national scale, not just in the north. This would involve considerable investment and even longer working hours but the two brothers were resolute. With a new management team on board around the two brothers, Eddie Stobart really started to explode.

Edward was not famous for his flexibility, this was a very focused and driven individual, but he had somehow been able to make the transformation from a one-man workaholic into a skilled delegator. With William alongside him, they were a potent team. However, what the two brothers possessed in ambition and drive they still lacked in a massive contract, one that would mirror the grandiose ambitions they shared for their firm. That was, until 1987…

The Cumbrian firm Metal Box was a global power in the canning industry. Stobart had worked for them sporadically over the years since that first phone call at Christmas 1976 asking for help. By their own admission, Stobart in the mid-to-late 1980s was still not the most prominent haulage firm in the northwest; even so, when Edward heard that Metal Box were looking for an exclusive contract with one haulier but were not even going to ask Stobart to tender (because Metal Box considered his firm too small), he was furious. Spurred on by his fierce ambition and the pride he had in doing better than any rivals, he simply called up Metal Box and kept them on the phone, gradually starting to win them round. He requested the complex tender forms and when this hefty paperwork was duly received, he worked around the clock for three days to complete his proposal in time. He knew the scale of the contract was actually almost beyond his company but to make

Above: *Stobart drivers have even been known to stay late on Christmas Eve to clean their trucks.*

Above: *A Ford Cargo: one of 25 bought after securing the Metal Box contract.*

sure Metal Box didn't think the same he stated that he had 70 trucks, not 50 as was actually the case. With this slight bending of the truth, Edward made his pitch on time and won a contract that would prove to be a major turning point in the firm's history. The number of loads that Stobart lorries were carrying doubled overnight.

William now looks back on securing the 1987 Metal Box contract as a massive watershed moment; it had also been a considerable risk. 'Despite the growth in the company, it wasn't really happening at that point. We were working through other hauliers up until then. There were these so-called "clearing houses" where brokers would collate the work and pass it on to different hauliers. These clearing houses were all over England but you struggled getting paid, and you didn't always get a good rate.

'We made a decision that in the future we were only going to work for customers direct. For the size we were, that was quite unusual, but me and me brother felt that we had to make that stand… and it was the best thing we ever did. It was a risk because other hauliers wouldn't work with you afterwards because you were "customer-direct", but we held firm. It could have killed the business altogether, it was a gamble, because instead of all being together with the hauliers around you, we were pulling away.' The tension was exacerbated by a steelworkers' strike around this time that left Stobart having to put drivers on 'two days on, two days off. That was a tough time,' recalls William.

The stress and workload were made worse by Edward's exaggerated fleet numbers which had helped secure the contract: 'Overnight we needed 25 more trucks!' recalls William, 'but we didn't have them. We'd sort of sold ourselves to Metal Box that we had more trucks than we had, so now we had to change numbers on the trailers to make it look like we were bigger than we actually were. We quickly got some finance together and bought 25 Ford Cargos, which was the biggest single order the dealership in Carlisle had ever received. With these excellent 250 Cummins engines these trucks were doing a mile a gallon more than conventional trucks that other people used, and yet they were only two-thirds of the price. So we somehow managed to deliver on the Metal Box contract perfectly, that was such a big turning point.'

This investment in 25 new trucks (and the drivers) was a huge risk for Eddie Stobart, because the Metal Box contract wasn't a long-term agreement; if their service wasn't up to scratch the contract might not be renewed, which would have left the firm massively exposed to huge overheads and debt. 'It was simple really: we had to impress and make it work,' says William. They obviously did because, decades later, Stobart still runs this contract.

With Metal Box secured and the direct business model established, an energised Edward relentlessly scoured Britain for new contracts, hungrily chasing new business while William ran the office back at HQ. It was a powerful team. Another big move was when they opened their first depot outside of Cumbria, in Burnaston, Derbyshire – meaning Eddie Stobart was now beginning to gain access to the whole of the UK.

The expansion continued at a frantic pace. Through much of the 1980s the company was growing at over twenty-five per cent a year. By 1990, helped by massive contracts such as Metal Box, the firm had two hundred vehicles and was turning over £16 million across four depots.

Yet still Edward's ambition burned brightly. When he'd previously acquired 25 trucks, he immediately wanted 50; when he got to 50 he wanted one hundred; then five hundred and then one thousand.

He still branded the lorries meticulously: the green had become darker and he'd added an orange-yellow detail as a third colour. In Edward's eyes, this branding was entirely for the trade – he knew that customers liked the idea of their goods being transported in spotless, beautifully painted trucks and at this

STAT//

WHEN BBC'S *TOP GEAR* LAUNCHED A RELIANT ROBIN INTO SPACE, THEY USED STOBART TO TRANSPORT THE CAR AND KIT TO THE FIRING-RANGE LAUNCH SITE. DESPITE THE ROCKET FAILING TO REACH ANYWHERE NEAR SPACE, IT WAS STILL THE BIGGEST NON-COMMERCIAL ROCKET LAUNCH EVER IN EUROPE.

//STAT

stage had no thought that the public might pick up on the image, as they later so famously did. Another crafty benefit of his trucks having such a bold presence on the roads of Britain was that when Edward was in negotiations with large firms for huge contracts, if he did perhaps 'exaggerate' the size of his fleet then potential customers would usually accept his numbers happily, given that his lorries were so conspicuous on the roads.

To reinforce this professional pride, in 1987 Edward introduced uniforms to the fleet of drivers. This was almost unheard of at the time. Some larger firms might have had the occasional branding in small letters on boiler suits, but by and large the image of truck drivers was still quite scruffy and unkempt. They were often foul-mouthed and could be heard bad-mouthing their bosses in cafes across the country. Edward refused to accept this as the norm and was convinced that a uniformed driver would further increase the feeling that his haulage firm was the best. He wanted to instil a sense of 'professional pride' into his drivers. So he supplied basic green jackets and trousers for them. 'People were just wearing boiler suits back then,' recalls William. 'So it was a new idea. There was usually no branding associated with the company.'

Once the Eddie Stobart tradition of wearing uniforms was established, it quickly became an essential part of the brand's image. In the August 1990 launch issue of the in-house magazine, *Stobart Express*, the high-profile decision to add shirts and ties to the original basic uniform of a jacket and trousers was announced: 'The uniform approach to smartness has just been taken a step further. All personnel who were previously issued with the Stobart work jacket and trousers now get matching shirts and ties to wear every working day. It's all part of the company's drive to maintain a clean and smart image.' The personnel administrator, Sheila Woodbridge, was quoted saying: 'Our drivers are our ambassadors and their image is just as important as our vehicles' image.' The shirts, available in long or sort sleeves, had embroidered pockets and the ties were polyester with a Stobart motif.

The article also said, 'Personnel must wear them on duty – and so far views have been favourable'. Sheila was further quoted saying, 'It's raised their profile and attracted attention to them, although some felt it would expose them to ridicule at first. Now they seem quite happy with the concept.'

'We were worried the tie was dangerous,' remembers William, 'which is why we made it clip-on. Mind you, that made you feel a bit like you were back at school!' The urban myth suggests that not wearing the tie was a sackable offence, and in theory it was if the rule was repeatedly ignored, but no driver was ever dismissed for this. When the uniforms were first introduced, only two out of two hundred drivers refused to wear them but they soon left the company. The ties were later dropped due to concerns about safety and also because many drivers simply found them too uncomfortable for a physical job. Nonetheless, the Eddie Stobart uniform was one of the single most important factors in establishing the brand nationally, and it remains crucial to this day. In fact, many drivers report that turning up at the Uniform Issue Office and collecting the smart clothing is one of the most exciting parts of getting the job! The legend of the truckers in ties still follows every Stobart driver around however, as most drivers are frequently asked, 'Where's your tie?'

Above: *Many new Stobart drivers find picking up their company uniforms an exciting ritual.*

Speaking to the media years later, Edward was proud of his decision on uniforms: 'The tie wasn't the important thing about the uniform,' he said. 'It was the discipline.' He also said, 'Transport had had a shifty image for a long time. The average truck driver or small operator was basically a tramp. Service in the industry needed to be upgraded, so we put in standards which others are now following.'

Edward's eagerness to introduce new standards to haulage became a founding tenet of the firm's success; his brother William complemented this by pouncing on any new technology that he felt could aid the business. One obvious – and massive – change from when William first started driving aged 21 has been the introduction of mobile phones: 'Before that, like when I started, it was all phone

Above: *Famously OCD driver Mark Dixon modelling Stobart's summer (top) and winter uniforms.*

boxes. I have spent hours and hours of my life inside phone boxes with 10p pieces! You used to spend your whole day planning where the phone boxes were, collecting bags of 10ps and then working out where the phone boxes were on your route. It wasn't as simple as that either, you also had to be able to park a 40-tonne artic nearby! That was usually very difficult so you got to know where the most convenient phone boxes were with all the best parking areas, but quite often so did all the other drivers!

'Once you'd finally parked up and got in the phone box, you'd call the office and they might be engaged! And of course once you got back in your wagon there was no way they could get hold of you if there was a problem. We even rang BBC Radio 2 once and asked them to put a message out for a driver we needed to contact urgently; they did, he heard it, stopped his truck and phoned us!'

It was with this inconvenient and inefficient phone-box culture in mind that William had bought one of the very first mobile phones to be sold in the UK. It was 1982 when he paid £1,200 for a Motorola: 'It was basically a car battery with a phone stuck to it! Even then there were only certain parts of the country it would work in, it worked in Carlisle but then it wouldn't work until you got to Glasgow so you would set off and lose signal almost straight away! But it was an amazing thing at the time.'

William had married in 1987 and soon had two young children to look after. Yet the business was demanding more and more of his time: 'It was earning money and doing well and we were growing. We were always very competitive on pricing, we had the right vehicles doing the right miles per gallon, and we had the right planners, so we were able to grow quickly. That said, I was just working day and night, basically!'

In 1992, Edward's father Eddie Stobart, now aged 63, suffered a particularly painful bout of shingles in the inner ear that was initially feared to be far more serious, potentially a brain tumour. This was a very frightening experience that made him reassess his work and social life. His deep faith completely overshadowed his interest in business by this time and so it was that on 15 December 1992 he resigned as Chairman of Eddie Stobart Ltd. His two sons Edward and William would spend the next decade turning a large local firm with national contracts into the highest-profile haulage firm ever seen in Great Britain.

In 1993, Eddie Stobart turned over £34 million; by 1997, that had rocketed to £102 million. In the same period their warehouse space had tripled and their fleet grown from three trucks to seven hundred. A year later that was eight hundred. By the summer of 1999, the nine-hundredth truck, Florence, arrived. The whole of the 1990s could be summed up in one word: growth.

Through that decade the firm was also a regular winner of numerous industry awards, including 'Haulier of the Year' and 'Marketer of the Year'. The company came to be seen as symbolic of British entrepreneurial brilliance, a status that was rewarded on 13 November 1997 when the firm's huge new Daventry depot was opened by HRH The Princess Royal. This was the jewel in Stobart's crown, a gargantuan site containing 500,000 square feet of warehouse space on opening day. There was even an on-site barber's! On that afternoon, The Princess Royal chatted with workers and spoke to the very first Eddie Stobart driver, Norman Bell. Such a royal stamp of approval was just the latest in a long line of recognitions and accomplishments for Britain's most famous haulage firm. As the decade closed, and both the new millennium and the firm's 30th anniversary approached, the growth continued unabated – by 2000 the company had more than 900 lorries and 22 depots, and their turnover had tripled in the previous five years alone. As they celebrated this success and the new era with the launch of their new website, the rampant success story that was Eddie Stobart seemed untouchable. //

Above: *A proud Edward presenting the new Daventry depot to HRH the Princess Royal in 1997 (top) and collecting another industry award.*

Bears, Books and Badges

WHILE FOOTBALLERS, SINGERS AND ACTORS ARE FETED BY THE PUBLIC, SO TOO IS THE RED-AND-GREEN FLEET OF EDDIE STOBART TRUCKS; HOW HAS THIS HAPPENED? THE FAN CLUB, THE 'EDDIE SPOTTERS', THE GIRLS' NAMES, THE MERCHANDISE... THE CULT OF EDDIE STOBART.

Edward Stobart always made it his priority to have clean, well-maintained and beautifully liveried trucks. He saw this as vital to keep his customers reassured that their goods were being shipped in the cleanest, most up-to-date and safe vehicles. As already noted, during the 1980s and 1990s the firm was expanding at a remarkable rate; as the 1990s ended, it seemed only a matter of time before the company bought its thousandth truck, a staggering statistic. Nonetheless, despite this exponential growth, Edward refused to let standards slip.

Britain's Best Known Road Haulage Company

EDDIE STOBART *Fan Club* NEWS

Your all new Fan Club Magazine . . .

ISSUE 1 SPRING 1997

THE FIRST EVER!

Since its launch in 1992 the Eddie Stobart Fan Club has grown from a few eager 'Spotters' in to a huge organisation with thousands of members throughout Europe.

Welcome to the very first issue of The Eddie Stobart Fan Club News - it's a magazine just for you, our fans, and it wouldn't have been possible without your fantastic support.

There's something for everyone inside - with a selection of your photographs and drawings as well as poems.

You can win one of our fabulous Tekno Scale Models and update your 'Spotter Manual' with the latest additions to the fleet - there are some Extra Special Offers for Fan Club Members and some great new models to collect - I hope you enjoy your magazine and keep sending us your pictures, poems and letters as well as suggestions for forthcoming issues.

Edward Stobart
Chairman and Chief Executive Eddie Stobart Ltd.

Pamela Jayne - the only girl in Lee's life...

Carlisle born Lee Brennan of chart toppers *'911'* is an 'Eddie Spotter' with a difference

After leaving school, one of Lee Brennan's first jobs was with the sign company which produced and fitted the famous Eddie Stobart livery to the company's fleet, and now on his travels between shows all over Britain and Europe not only is Lee a keen 'Eddie Spotter' but he takes great delight in spotting the trucks he worked on.

Lee says - " It's great to be reminded of home especially when you don't get back there as often as you would like, when we fly back in from a gig on the continent one of the first things we usually see is an Eddie Stobart truck, which is a nice reminder of home."

"I used to apply all the girls names to the front of the trucks so I do know a lot of them personally - at the time it was hard work - each one had to be perfect, occasionally we had to work through the night on new trucks it took about three hours to apply the transfers to each cab and trailer and sometimes we had six lined up to be done - now I see them on the roads all over Europe and I get a real buzz if I see one of mine"!

With the release of 911's debut album appropriately titled 'The Journey' - it looks like Lee and the boys will be doing a lot of Eddie Spotting during the next few weeks.

WIN THIS SUPERB TEKNO ERF SCALE MODEL

Above: *Eddie Bear. He does not currently hold an HGV Class 1 licence.*

These years were staggeringly successful for Stobart as a business but away from the burgeoning fleet, impressive turnover figures, expansive profits and industry recognition, something very strange started to happen... something very strange indeed.

'We started getting a trickle of letters from members of the public,' recalls William Stobart. 'Obviously we had the girls' names on each truck but unbeknown to us, the public had started noticing this.' At first, these letters were dealt with by Edward's secretary Debbie Rodgers, who would simply write back and say thanks for the interest. Edward insisted that every one was answered in turn. His theory was that each one of these letters might be from someone who could potentially be a future customer so they all had to be respected and replied to.

As the trickle of letters increased, a pattern emerged among the questions being asked. 'Was it a real person's name on the side of the lorries?' 'Why were the girls' names picked?' 'Who picked them?' 'Could they get their daughters'/wives'/mothers' names on a lorry?' 'Was Eddie Stobart a real person?' These and other repeated questions eventually led Debbie to create a fact sheet that she could then post back with each reply. Initially this was simply a photocopied list and, if requested, she might also send another photocopy detailing the fleet list, as used by the firm itself. She soon started enclosing a calendar or sometimes a pen, small gifts which the company had originally intended only for corporate use.

In August 1990, the company had published the first issue of *Stobart Express*, a four-page in-house and trade publication designed to be sent out to all employees and customers in order to keep them up to date with the latest developments at the firm. Soon, copies of this quarterly magazine were also being included in the replies to 'fan' letters.

That first issue of *Stobart Express* gives a fascinating insight into the mindset of Edward and the company at that time – and hints at the down-to-earth nature of the Stobarts and their inherent work ethic that has made them so popular with the fans, known as Spotters. In his opening article, Edward said, 'It could have been easy to lose touch. We have tried to not let that happen... we are all part of the Stobart team and the way we each do our job affects the rest of the team... We hope the newsletter will be a bit of fun, but it's also an important way of keeping everyone in touch with the heart of the business.'

If you had received this magazine as a Spotter way back in 1990, then as well as the words by Edward, the first issue detailed contracts and company news, a competition and a charity bike ride by one of the staff. There was also an interview with 'Operations Director' William Stobart, who explained how the fleet was rarely running empty trailers and gave details of the vehicles, including 'a mixed fleet of Volvos, Seddon Atkinson, Scania, Ford Cargo, some Iveco, Mercedes and DAFs.' The vehicles all had 'the latest in cell-phone technology in the cab, so that the planners can stay in constant touch.' There was also a feature on Debbie Rodgers, the Spotters' first point of contact.

Soon, the cult of Eddie Spotters ramped up a notch with the first 'celebrity' fan, jazz musician Jools Holland. In 1991, that star's PA wrote in requesting a Stobart calendar, explaining that Jools's touring band had regularly 'spotted' the trucks up and down the motorways while on tour and the calendar would make a nice parting gift now that the concerts had come to an end. Holland went on to mention his fascination with Stobart lorries in a prominent *Sunday Times* interview and that, along with a reader's letter printed in the *Sun*, saw the momentum of this unexpected 'fan' following begin to snowball even further. (Many years later, in July 2010, William Stobart presented Jools Holland with a model truck backstage at a concert at Carlisle racecourse as a gesture of thanks; he also gave him a celebrity membership pack so he could carry on spotting!)

STAT//

IN SERIES TWO OF BBC COMEDY *GAVIN & STACEY*, THE CHARACTER NESSA JENKINS SAYS THAT SHE WAS A DRIVER FOR EDDIE STOBART LTD AND THAT SHE KNEW EDWARD HIMSELF VERY WELL.

//STAT

Every week more letters kept arriving and delving a little further revealed the extent of their fascination: there were various scoring systems used, with extra points being awarded for unusually named trucks, completely new names, rare vehicles, and so on.

The problem was that obviously Eddie Stobart had never intended this to happen – it was just a haulage firm! Nonetheless, the trickle became a tidal wave and by the end of 1991, the cost of posting replies to the growing surge of fan letters was over £5,000. The volume of letters was further increased when the firm won the prestigious 'Haulier of the Year' Award in 1992.

In response to this unexpected wave of letters, in the spring of 1992 the Eddie Stobart fan club was formed. Members got a car sticker and a newsletter in return for a small annual fee. That very first newsletter published a selection of drawings and photos by fans, as well as poems. Competitions to win model trucks were complemented by a Spotter's Manual and member special offers. Incredibly, within two years the fan club had 10,000 members and the momentum moved up another notch when Stobart struck a deal with *Corgi* to manufacture scale replicas of their lorries. Only weeks after their launch, these trucks were one of Corgi's best-selling lines. The Corgi toys first went on sale in December 1992 at many service stations and toy shops around the UK.

In 1999, the fan club newsletter and the firm's separate in-house magazine *Stobart Express* were merged into a brand-new lavishly printed seasonal publication entitled *Spot On*, which is a bible for all Eddie Spotters worldwide.

This intense interest in the fan club and products such as the Corgi trucks highlighted a fascination from the fans that went beyond merely spotting trucks up and down the motorways. Suddenly Stobart were presented with a viable new way of making money – just as with any modern celebrity, the fans wanted merchandise. Over the years, Eddie Stobart has not disappointed; there has been a bewildering array of merchandise. At the time of writing, the catalogue offers

offers caps, boxer shorts, hoodies, T-shirts, shirts, Polo neck shirts, socks, pyjamas, fleeces, beanies, raincoats, baby-gro's, slippers, mugs, pencil cases and extensive amounts of stationery, a tax disc holder, numerous bags, mouse mats, wallets, bins, kids' activity books, keyrings. Wallpaper, duvets, air freshener… the list goes on.

In June 1997 the company opened a Stobart fan club shop in Carlisle Street in the city, aiming to 'provide our fans with the full array of Stobart merchandise under one roof – and to add to the city's tourist attractions.' This was eventually moved to the Carlisle depot, which is where it currently resides.

By the turn of the new century, Stobart's image had progressed to that of a genuine 'national treasure' – one of the UK's best-loved and most visible brands. The company responded by expanding its merchandising activities into a substantial children's multi-media project called Steady Eddie. In his first incarnation, Steady was a 2D animated truck, complete with his own cartoon, adventure books and road safety campaign. A decade on, Steady Eddie has been completely re-invented for a new generation of children.

Now a fully animated 3D boy with a distinctive quiff, Steady Eddie has his own futuristic transport company, complete with control tower, multi-modal HQ and environmental message (which his arch enemy Terry of old-style Horrid Haulage battles at every turn). From late 2012, Steady Eddie and his trusty crew of lorries, trains, boats and planes were introduced to children and parents across the UK ensuring happier journeys – thanks to lorry-tracking Apps, in-car games, activity books, a fanzine and Steady Eddie's very own Kid's Club – launched at Stobart Fest in Manchester.

Above: *Steady Eddie is back! Stobart have relaunched the popular character as a boy who owns a haulage company.*

Opposite: *From the first Corgi scale models in 1992, replica Stobart vehicles have been one of the firm's best-selling items of merchandise.*

There is an urban myth that at one point the fan club was making more money than the haulage firm – nonsense, of course, as Stobart Promotions sales in 2011 were an impressive £800,000 whereas the whole group turned over more than half a billion. But nonetheless the more colourful side of Stobart has allowed the business to venture into newer areas. The title of one of these books, *Hedgehog Crossing*, also hinted at another way Eddie Stobart has used the fan base to diversify, in this case into charitable causes. In 2004 the fan club started a 'Spike and Eddie' campaign to raise awareness of the plight of hedgehogs, raising money for CRASH – Care, Rehabilitation and Aid for Sick Hedgehogs – complete with a 'hedgehog hospital that takes 2000 patients a year'. Spike was a cuddly hedgehog toy, complete with a red baseball cap with the company's 'S' logo on the front, retailing for £5, of which £1 went to CRASH.

Another similar venture was the launch of exclusive teddy bears that were named to coincide with each new lorry added to the fleet. The beautifully made Eddie bears featured a solid silver engraved button sewn into the ear, and the name of the new truck and the year embroidered on the paw pad. The bears each had an Eddie Stobart fleece jacket and baseball cap with logo. The bear was offered first to the person who had named the truck, all with the intention of raising funds for children's cancer charities, with 10 per cent of the £85 price tag being donated.

In May 2002, excited Spotters would have seen a convoy of Stobart trucks heading up to Blackpool Pleasure Beach. These were only 'toy' trucks however, on the way to the pleasure beach for the launch of the so-called Eddie Stobart Convoy Track.

This fairground ride was created with exacting detail: just like the real thing, the trucks all had girls' names, including Queenie, Measha, Sandie, Hannah and Shelley. Hannah was named after Hannah Brown, aged four at that time, who suffered from congenital cardiomyopathy, a terminal condition. This is another welcome example of the massive amount of charity work that Eddie Stobart has

done over the years. Edward himself later invited little Hannah to a depot where she had a great day out meeting drivers and sitting in trucks.

Back at Blackpool for the launch of the Convoy ride, Edward was also present to squeeze into the miniature trucks to celebrate the opening of the ride. Bottles of champagne were popped and curvaceous models bedecked in the firm's colours were photographed by the press pack. No attention to detail was missed, with the ticket collector even wearing an authentic Eddie Stobart uniform.

The fan interest in the company is very much a two-way relationship. While Stobart offer fun ventures such as Steady Eddie, the fairground ride, depot visits and all the merchandise, the fanbase is now so active that the company is swamped by thousands of drawings, letters, posters and other fan mail every week. A trawl through the archive of the fan club newsletters reveals one fan who made an Eddie Stobart weather vane in the shape of a truck; another Spotter made an Eddie truck bed for his young son, in precise detail; another young fan named his Cocker Spaniel Eddie Stobart which his father revealed was the cause of much confusion whenever the dog was taken to the vet's and his name was shouted out! During one particularly white Christmas, a young girl made, then photographed, an Eddie 'Sto-man'; another fan who ran a car-repair business in Tyne and Wear painted his Mini car in Stobart livery while yet another inventive fan painted his remote control plane in the famous colours. Fans regularly send in cakes in the shape of lorries; in fact, so many cakes are made that the fan club magazine started printing a dedicated page for photographs of these delicious dedications, simply called 'The Cake Shop'.

Sometimes the fans are famous themselves – we've seen how Jools Holland was perhaps the earliest famous face to follow Eddie, but since then former Boyzone singer Ronan Keating has revealed he also counts the trucks while on tour. Kerry Katona has a truck named after her (Kerry Jayne) and when the firm sent a picture of the truck named after Elvis Presley's former wife, Priscilla, to the latter's US address, she replied saying that it was an 'honour to be on your truck' and said she had put the photo in her office. One celebrity who wasn't a fan was Philip Schofield, who said the company calendar for 1994 was 'the most boring' he'd seen and even held it up on camera during his *Going Live* TV show!

Other famous Spotters reportedly include: Shane Lynch (another ex-Boyzone star), British rally champion Mark Higgins, Radio 2's Sally Boazman and Johnny Walker, Keith Chegwin, Fiona Phillips, Roxanne Pallett from *Emmerdale*; *Coronation Street*'s Alan Halsall, Brian Capron, Simon Gregson and Suranne Jones, Radio 1 DJ Chris Moyles and *Bullseye* presenter Jim Bowen. Tony Blair's youngest son, Leo, used to play with Eddie Stobart miniature lorries in 10 Downing Street.

There are other, more bizarre celebrity connections. Pop star Lee Brennan of 1990s' act 911 used to work at the signwriters who put the girls' names on the front. And sometimes the celebrities are moved to more than just letter writing. Eddie Spotters the world over always chant 'Eddie Stobart' to the tune of the 'Hallelujah' chorus, but in 1995 The Wurzels took this musical adoration one step further, and released the song 'I Want to be an Eddie Stobart Driver'. The tune was written by Titcombe/Barker and reached the lofty heights of No. 96 in the charts. You could even get the song as a ringtone! At the time, the Eddie Stobart in-house magazine rather optimistically suggested, 'What better way to impress your friends?!' Later, a spoof version called 'I Wanna Join the Eddie Stobart Fan Club' was made available for download. The music connection was reignited in the early 2000s when the company ran a 'premier music talent search' called The Stobart Factor.

The relationship between Stobart and the fans remains very close. The depot tours are hugely popular and the more dedicated Spotters are known personally to most drivers. Each depot where spotting is allowed has designated Spotter Areas to

Above: *The famously private Edward Stobart opens the Convoy ride at Blackpool Pleasure Beach.*

//STAT

AT THE TIME OF WRITING, TO FILL UP PHOEBE GRACE WITH 450 LITRES OF DIESEL WOULD COST IN THE REGION OF £625.

ensure both personal safety and the best view! The biggest depots are Appleton in Warrington and Crick in the Midlands (known as The Glass House because of its striking architecture) but it is the latter, along with Carlisle (where it all started) that are the two most popular depots. Crick is very central, very busy (over 250 trucks a day pass through this sixty-acre site) and therefore a popular place for Spotters to see drivers park up, get refuelled and take a break.

Whenever a new truck arrives, there is a flurry of interest from the Spotters; should a new type of truck be purchased – such as a fuel tanker or a biomass truck – this adds an extra frisson of hysteria. When the company bought a state-of-the-art Volvo FH16 in 2010, complete with the personalised number plate S708 ART, a gaggle of Spotters were there to welcome the truck and driver Matt Ekin on its first drive. There are league tables for the fans to compete in (2000 are registered) and some of the top Spotters have signed off on over 5000 trucks over the years. A 'spot' is only counted when the vehicle is commissioned into service and in full ESL or customer livery; the three distinctive pieces of information which Spotters collect are registration, fleet number and name – along with the make of vehicle and where it has been seen. The league table is regularly updated on the website and there is also a *Spotter's Journal* where avid followers can upload recent sightings.

There have even been a couple of isolated incidents of 'Spotter rage' when competition to spot new trucks got a little overheated. On a lighter note, fans regularly get married in front of the trucks and even sometimes drive off from their ceremony in the lorries. On one occasion a baby – the daughter of a truck-magazine editor – was taken to her christening in a Stobart truck.

At the time of writing, the membership stands at 20,000 and includes fans from all over the world, including Holland, Germany, Ukraine, the Far East and even Australasia! For your annual membership fee you get a personal membership card, an enamel lapel badge, an official member's sticker, a fleet list detailing every vehicle name, number and type in the *Spotter's Guide*, an exclusive Eddie Stobart calendar and copies of *Spot On*. You also get access to exclusive 'Members Only' areas of the website where you can register your spotting achievements and use a fleet search engine. The site also leads you to www.stobartgames.com where there is an on-line game called Drawbar Derby. Perhaps the most prized member's gift is the hallowed *Spotter's Handbook*, printed biannually, which includes an explanation of the various trucks and trailers as

Above: *The Eddie Stobart fan club has more than 20,000 enthusiastic members.*

well as fleet numbers and names, ready to be ticked off when spotted on the roads. More frequent fleet updates can be accessed online.

For the drivers, the Spotters certainly add a unique element to their trucking work. They never know when a Spotter will toot their horn or wave or come over for a photograph; when one trucker drove to John O'Groats and took a tea break at the northernmost point of the UK, no sooner was he parked up than an Eddie Spotter came over and asked for a photograph.

It is a fact that drivers are supposed to respond in kind – with a honk of the horn too – should a Spotter wave at them, and generally most do. 'We always try to wave back, of course,' explains well-known driver Mark Dixon, 'but sometimes you physically can't. I'm in charge of a massive truck and if I'm going round a roundabout when someone waves, I need to keep total control of that 44-tonne lorry first, and wave second!'

The names on the trucks remain the single most important element to any self-respecting Spotter, followed by the fleet number. The top Spotters will already know that the longest truck name to date is Gladys Duchess of Overton while the shortest are Nia, Pia and Una. There is an international delegation, too:

'Tuula Karina' (Finnish), 'Angharrad' (Welsh), 'Anstice' and 'Saoirse Erin' (Irish). Most Spotters were surprised, some horrified, when the firm named one truck Valentino after the men's MotoGP world champion Valentino Rossi. There was also a truck called Optimus Prime, christened to celebrate the Transformers' twentieth anniversary, while elsewhere in the Stobart Group there are the Eddie and Bart engines from the rail division. Otherwise it is strictly only girls allowed. Notably, some drivers even call their sat-navs by girls' names!

The queue to name a truck after someone special carries a three-year wait. There are a few special exceptions such as when the then-Conservative Party leader William Hague had a vehicle named after his wife Ffion in 1998. Another lucky lady won the right to have the sparkling new FH16 truck named after her – Debby – when her property developer partner paid £5,000 for the privilege at an auction in London's Battersea Power Station, as part of the company's glitzy fortieth anniversary celebrations.

At Battersea, the sides of the trailer were also auctioned off, with 156 people paying £1,000 each to have their name down one side, while the opposite side was cheekily bought by rival haulage firm Malcolm's; Stobart got into the charity spirit though and duly had their rival's logo put on one of their own trailers, all for a good cause. The fund-raising didn't stop there: Mark Dixon appeared on stage to hand over a cheque for £151,700 – which was the 2010 revenue from his truck, Phoebe Grace.

The extent to which Eddie Stobart had become a 'celebrity' was clear to see in 2011 at the first (soon-to-be-annual) Stobart Fest, which took place at Rockingham Raceway in Northamptonshire. Remarkably, more than 7,000 people turned up to see the fifteen trucks on show and meet a selection of drivers. At this event, the winner of another competition to name a truck was also announced. The competition was first launched at Truckfest in Peterborough in 2010, and for each month of the year, the company had placed one truck on the road without a

Above: *Andrew Tinkler meets Eddie fans at a Stobart Fest.*

name, bearing instead just a question mark. If spotted, the fleet number and location had to be noted and registered online for a chance to win the prize. At the 2012 Stobart Fest, in the grounds of Manchester City FC's Etihad Stadium, thousands of Eddie fans swarmed around the trucks in baking sunshine, with queues to meet the drivers stretching into hundreds of people. This was bona fide celebrity worship.

The massed ranks of Eddie Spotters remain an essentially bizarre phenomenon: a fan club of a haulage firm. In the modern age of celebrity, singers, sportsmen and actors all have thousands of fans following their every move. But Eddie Stobart is, at its core, a haulage firm, not a celebrity. Surprisingly, other haulage firms also have fan clubs and spotters too (see www.lorryspotters.com!) but none are anywhere near as big or high-profile as Eddie Stobart.

Clearly using girls' names was a massively crucial element; prior to this lorries were just big, oily, noisy vehicles that slowed down your journey. Giving each truck a feminine name humanised them and turned the slow traffic of Britain's roads into an entertaining game. The Corgi toys were not just popular with kids to actually buy – they also made the real lorries on the roads look more like benign gigantic toys, trundling along our motorways like some real-life kids' cartoon, again demystifying and humanising them. I asked William Stobart why he thought this surprising turn of events had happened: 'Eddie Stobart is a very "personal" name, if you know what I mean. It caught the imagination, even though for us it was just a massive billboard going down the motorway. Then we had the girls' names on the trucks, plus the drivers were in the shirts and ties, and the combination of all that just attracted attention. People just seem to love the trucks.'

The result? A branding phenomenon. //

SPOTTER'S HANDBOOK

This hallowed booklet is the bible for all Eddie Spotters. The Introduction offers a few insights into 'What to look for' as well as a list of livery codes. Each truck has a girl's name but there are also a series of identifying numbers, used for operational reasons. Low down on the cab is also the truck's fleet number, below the name, used to identify the type of vehicle.

F	RIGID		**L**	LIGHT
H	ARTIC		**X**	SHUNT
M	ROAD TRAIN		**T**	TESCO
V	VAN		**RV**	RAIL VEHICLE

Eddie Stobart
Spotter's Handbook
18th Special Diamond Jubilee Edition

The complete official listing of the famous Eddie Stobart fleet as of August 2012

Dark Days and New Horizons

DIFFICULT TIMES AND THE TRAGIC, PREMATURE LOSS OF EDWARD STOBART, FOLLOWED BY A STAGGERING REJUVENATION THAT SAW EDDIE STOBART RECLAIM ITS CROWN AS BRITAIN'S GREATEST TRANSPORT COMPANY.

By the end of the 1990s, Eddie Stobart was one of the biggest haulage firms in the UK; it was certainly the best known, with a huge fan club and a thriving sideline in merchandise. The fleet was always expanding and, on the surface, business looked very good. Largely due to this enormous success, Eddie Stobart has over the years been the subject of many rumours. Various 'Eddie's going bust' whispers have resonated through the haulage industry on more than one occasion but none proved correct. That said, by the turn of 2003, the company was actually facing financial dire straits. For once, the rumours about difficulties were not just spiteful gossip instigated by rivals.

In retrospect, the first signs of difficulties might have been when the firm announced that they would not be present at the annual pilgrimage for all haulage firms and truck fans, Truckfest, in 1999. Their high-profile absence was stated as being because 'we now find our time fully occupied by lobbying government at the highest level and impressing upon them the importance of the British road haulage industry'. This protest came following changes to fuel and road tax that Stobart felt compromised their competitiveness against European hauliers. Coincidence perhaps? Or cost-cutting? What wasn't open to speculation was that in 2002 Eddie Stobart posted its first ever loss.

There were other, sadder factors at play too. Edward's marriage had failed in 1996 – no doubt partially exacerbated by his legendary work ethic – and he was still reluctantly the very public face of what was now a huge business empire. Speaking to writer Hunter Davies for his magnificent 2002 book, Edward himself did acknowledge that his success had sometimes come at a hefty personal price but he explained that he felt he had little choice – the firm must either expand or risk becoming uncompetitive, and he wanted to provide for his family.

This is a man who had somehow been able to operate this huge logistics operation almost entirely from his head for years, writing very little down. For the first 29 years, the company didn't even have board meetings – Edward would phone in from a truck and tell everyone what was going on! However, the modern age required a mass of technology and structure that no longer allowed this enigmatic and individualistically brilliant approach to continue.

Edward had made a personal fortune and he enjoyed the fruits of his labours. He had a beautiful house and a Ferrari on the drive. He personally helped dig out a four-acre lake in his grounds, taking days completing the work in a JCB which he loved every minute of. He even bought a luxury yacht at one point but there was the sense that these material things meant little to him compared to the success of his business, that was always his overwhelming obsession. Eventually he sold the Ferrari and the yacht. He also sold any personal number plates he had because he was never comfortable being recognised by the public.

William Stobart was still working tirelessly alongside Edward during these more difficult times. 'I was Operating Director basically. I ran all the transport and all the planners we had, the whole operation, while Edward did the customers and the accounts side. The relationship was always great but towards the end of the 1990s me brother was more difficult to handle for various reasons. He had some personal issues and we felt we wanted to take the business in different directions; he wasn't into IT or systems or procedures, and in the past it had

Above: *For Edward Stobart, the success of his trucks was far more important than his own, unwanted personal celebrity.*

been very much a case of what he said went, he was very much a one-man show.'

Edward was always a very private individual, wary of strangers – perhaps a legacy of his childhood stammer? – and wasn't enamoured of big social functions; despite his firm's success he was rarely seen in the media but in some ways this just added to the mystique. This intense private side was part of the unusual paradox that the essentially very public figure Edward Stobart lived. At one point he started buying petrol for his personal car with cash as he didn't like people seeing his name on credit cards and asking him questions. He wanted success for his business; fame meant nothing to him.

Meanwhile, William's brother-in-law and best friend Andrew Tinkler had his own hugely successful railway business – WA Developments – and in 2001 William decided to leave Stobart and buy a 27 per cent stake in Andrew's firm. 'I wanted to go me own path, go my own way and I just felt me brother was heading in the wrong direction. I told me brother what I'd done and there were a lot of arguments

//STAT

but he wouldn't buy me out of Stobart. Then around 2003 he was having a lot of issues with management, and to cut a long story short, in 2004 me and Andrew bought the company off him, a complete buyout. Basically the deal was done in one evening and we had the paperwork done within a fortnight and Edward went off to Portugal!'

William suggests that Edward needed assistance to run the huge business he had built up: 'He just couldn't manage it any more like it was, and it got to a point where it was losing money and he was going from fire-fighting to fire-fighting. We felt that if we hadn't done a deal that evening and took it over, you were talking a matter of weeks and it would have gone bankrupt.'

And so began the third phase in the remarkable story of Eddie Stobart. The first phase had been those early beginnings at the Newlands Hill farm, when the brothers had worked for their father who had built up the business from nothing. The second phase was when Edward transformed that agricultural contracting firm into an iconic haulage business with a multi-million pound turnover and a fan club whose membership ran into thousands. Now, the third phase was to see William and his best friend Andrew Tinkler take over the business and expand at an incredible rate into rail, air, sea and biomass, expanding the core haulage business into a so-called 'multi-modal' logistics model that at the time of writing turns over more than half a billion pounds a year.

Aside from the obvious personal sadness, William remains philosophical about the change of ownership: 'The company just needed focus and planning, it needed its customers back on board, it needed confidence. It didn't have that. It just needed a real good sort-out, so we made a few redundancies, we moved offices, we split the business up into smaller pockets operationally, we got back into working with the customers, we got a cost model that worked, a price that worked. Andrew brought the IT to it all, I've learned so much from the railway industry from Andrew, he's really good on IT and finance and spreadsheets and he was working every scenario out: he's a qualified engineer so it has to be exactly right! Fetching that dynamic into the transport industry really worked for us. Anybody else looking at that business from the outside would have really struggled, but I could go in straight away and manage it, which I did at the end of November 2003.'

And what did his older brother Edward do after selling the business in 2004? 'He had a lot of property investments and spent time in Portugal,' explains William, 'then he came back to England and kept in touch; he had no jealousy in him at all, he didn't have a nasty bone in his body. We had a lot of conversations at that time and he went off and invested in property. He still called me "boy" until I was about thirty; there was a time at the firm when no one knew me proper name!'

Sadly in 2010 Edward Stobart was declared bankrupt, as the global property market nose-dived. A far worse tragedy was to befall him and his family on 31 March 2011 when he died suddenly of heart problems. His family and the wider business community mourned the loss of an iconic figure. Hundreds of people packed Carlisle Cathedral for his funeral service, and scores of Spotters joined crowds on the street outside. Two of the pall-bearers were drivers with over thirty years' service each. The funeral was shown on big screens in the centre of Carlisle. As well as family and friends, the service was attended by former Boyzone singer Shane Lynch and *X Factor* finalist Rebecca Ferguson, who sang 'Amazing Grace' during the service. Carlisle United Football Club (sponsored by Stobart) sent a wreath with a tribute which read 'In memory of a great supporter'. A lorry-shaped wreath was among the floral tributes left outside the cathedral, while three Eddie Stobart trucks led the hearse away from Carlisle Cathedral.

In the summer, the company held an Edward Stobart Tribute Race Day at Newmarket, attended by many prominent business people and more than 500 Eddie Spotters (who were given free tickets by the company). The personal tragedy was obviously enormous – Edward left behind his second wife Mandy, their two kids and four adopted children from his first marriage to Sylvia. Those in the business

Above: *The crowds at Edward's funeral in 2011 reflected how well-known this private yet influential man had been.*

community soon speculated, did the famous haulage business still have a future?

Fortunately, after William Stobart and Andrew Tinkler took over in 2004, it quickly became apparent that with the two childhood friends at the helm, the business had never been stronger. The family firm is now home to over 5,500 employees running road, rail, air and ports. 'When we took over,' explains William, 'it was turning over more than £1 million a week, around £55 million a year, with around a thousand trucks. In 2011 we turned over £600 million and we have over 1,500 trucks. Haulage is about £450 million of that, so still the lion's share for now, but we are very excited about the new divisions.'

The two friends' insistence on investing for the future is staggering. For example, the year 2007 was a massive one for new trucks, with more than six hundred vehicles bought, including five hundred new Scanias. At £27 million, this was the largest order ever received by Scania UK. Stobart also ordered seven hundred trailers and celebrated the mammoth purchase with a special photo shoot at the Eiffel Tower in Paris. By 2007 the firm was back on such a solid footing that it was able to start acquiring other hauliers, such as James Irlam and O'Connor.

Also in the same year, the company won the prestigious 'Freight Achievement of the Year' Award, confirmation that Stobart was back at the top.

Officially there are five divisions in the Stobart Group: Transport and Distribution; Estates (representing their ever-growing number of property assets); Infrastructure and Civils (representing their work within the rail sector, civil engineering and other industries); Air; and Biomass.

The strategy since 2004 has been described as creating 'multimodal transport and logistics solutions'. This industry term is best explained by the firm's CEO, Andrew Tinkler. As previously explained, Andrew had made his fortune in the railway industry with his firm WA Developments. However, chatting to Andrew about his childhood and early adulthood, then the evolution of his career and the business principles he holds dear, sheds a very revealing light on the ethos and expertise that he brought to the business when he and William took over Stobart.

'To be fair, school probably wasn't my favourite subject,' Andrew suggests, modestly. 'But I had to go there anyway! I left at 16 and down the road from where I lived there were a joiner's shop, a cabinet maker, so I went in there and got an apprenticeship. I was always good with me hands. I did that for two or three years and then decided I wanted a change. Well, they were putting a gas pipeline through Cumbria at the time so I went and become a labourer for about six months. Then after that I went to work for Eddie Stobart.'

At the time – this is the early 1980s – Stobart had around 23 trucks. 'I knew William as a friend and that was how I come across getting the job. He told me they were looking for somebody to go into the garage, to wash trucks and maintain them. It was a bit of a change from joinery but I thought, Might as well give it a go! I was only 18, so I went to Carlisle and did that, washing the trucks and maintaining them in the day and I got into spraying them as well, painting them. I did that for about a year or so. It was a job, I did it and I enjoyed it. Eddie was good to be around, at the end of the day he was very much involved at that time and would even come and help us wash

STAT//

STOBART HAVE OVER 2,250 'TRACTOR UNITS' – ASSUMING AN AVERAGE OF 450BHP PER TRACTOR UNIT, THAT'S APPROXIMATELY A FLEET TOTAL OF IN EXCESS OF ONE MILLION HORSEPOWER.

Above: *Childhood friends William Stobart and Andrew Tinkler, who have transformed the company's fortunes since taking over in 2004.*

trucks as well! I come across William quite a bit each day, especially when I was washing his truck and I missed a bit, you always knew about it then!'

Andrew's restless instinct to learn moved him on from Stobart after twelve months. 'Once I'd done something for a while, I wanted to be on to summat else, so I was always looking for new opportunities. When you are young you don't look to settle down straightaway, so I was hungry for work.' He worked in joinery again, then farming and livestock. 'Then I went to work for Everest double-glazing and, to be fair, that was a very interesting job because that's where I really learned about making money. You were only paid for the jobs you did, not by the hour. I also learned about customer service; they had a policy in place that if you had to go back to repair something, Everest would take £20 off you, but if the customer wrote in and said you'd done a really good job, then they'd give you an extra £20. It was a bonus for doing a good job and delivering good customer service.

'All the time I was getting an underpinning of knowledge of all these aspects of business. So looking back it was probably pretty natural that I wanted to start me own business. I was always buying cars and messing about with them, which meant I had a bit of money, so I bought a Transit from the local butcher, put me joinery tools in the back and became a joiner and building contractor. That was 1987 so I was just 23. My first job was fitting a door on an old folk's home.'

This was also the year that Eddie Stobart secured that crucial Metal Box contract which William has said was a pivotal turning-point in the company's fortunes. For Andrew too, business was about to get a lot more successful... very quickly. 'The customer who owned the old folk's home fell out with his builder and he asked me if I wanted to work on the build – this eventually turned out to be a £400,000 job.'

Andrew soon needed employees and his reputation for meticulous work quickly attracted a host of lucrative contracts. Within a short time he was building housing projects, then large civil engineering jobs on the roads. Around this time, Railtrack (later known as Network Rail) were looking for contractors and Andrew tendered for and went on to win several large contracts. 'I went from £600,000 turnover to £26 million in three years. The opportunity was there, I had very good people around me – I always make sure of that – and it worked.

'I learned from early doors to put systems in place from the bottom right up. We had got good systems because I understood what was happening at shop level, right the way through, and them systems have served us well. Even today, I believe heavily in having a system and procedure in place for people to work from.'

Andrew recalls the period when he and William bought out Edward: 'We had to be sure the business was recoverable. The skill sets between William and meself worked really well. He had great knowledge of transport and I was looking to investigate the business and see where the problems were. In the first year we got it back to a break-even point. It was a risk but we did an extensive Risk Assessment beforehand and we believed we could recover the business. It was a lot of hard work at the time… mind you, it still is today!'

In the same way that the young Andrew Tinkler was always looking to try something new for a job, by the 2000s the experienced businessman was keen to expand Stobart's horizons, a strategy fully endorsed by, and created with, William. 'At that time, I'd come from a civil engineering background, William was from transport, fuel was becoming more and more expensive so it was clear we had to try to diversify. We wanted to develop an all-in-one transport solution whether it was road, rail, sea or air. Offering the full service to the customer and making absolutely sure their product is delivered on time.'

By 2007, the expansion plans were set and the potential was massive. 'We were growing the business but needed new investment so we looked around at various

//STAT

THE SO-CALLED SWING
DECK TRAILER HAS A CENTRE
PLATFORM THAT FOLDS
AWAY TO ALLOW FOR TALLER
LOADS. THESE DOUBLE-
DECKED DESIGNS CAN BE
CONVERTED INTO A STANDARD
UNIT CAPABLE OF HANDLING
TRADITIONAL PALLETISED LOADS
BY ONE MAN IN JUST A MATTER
OF MINUTES.

Opposite: *Andrew Tinkler's
extensive expertise in railway
logistics has helped Stobart to
expand into new markets.*

means of finance and decided to list the company on the Stock Market, as a PLC. That opened the door to investors and we could then go out there and really grow the business, we could make acquisitions – we bought some competitors, we bought a port, an airport, it's all part of providing a service. We want to be Number One in our field.'

Despite being the CEO of a multi-million pound operation, Andrew is still hungry for knowledge: 'I listen to everybody and everything and try to learn from it. Still do today. You haven't to get complacent, thinking you know everything because you don't and the more you listen the more you will succeed.'

Andrew doesn't feel that the Stock Market floatation has compromised Stobart's famous values whatsoever. 'Although it's a PLC it's still seen as a family business; the people are very loyal; some of them, if you cut them in half, they'd be green all the way through. They believe in the business and have been there a long time and they enjoy their jobs. There is a culture where they need to get on and deliver a service.

'Stobart is a household name and that fact really helps the business develop. A lot of the customers we do business with are actually Spotters themselves. They therefore recognise that the business is well known for delivering a great service, reliable and affordable, a good service provider.

'The plan for the future is to deliver shareholders' value and have the brand succeed in all the sectors we are in. Your brand is only as good as your last job and we never forget that. It's not all about money either, it's about succeeding in whatever you do, and everybody enjoying that success. I am driven and passionate about what I do – success makes me want to do more. But most importantly, this business is all about people, not just me or William, but all the people who work for us. In many ways it's all about those people.'

The breathtakingly comprehensive post-2004 strategy for the company's ambitious expansion has clearly worked. In addition to the fact that turnover

Opposite: *Stobart spend around £50-55 million each year on new trucks.*

has gone up to over half a billion pounds from £100 million in just seven years, there are any number of other facts and figures that endorse the compelling and expert approach made by William and Andrew. For example, in 1998, Eddie Stobart trucks used ten million gallons of diesel a year; in 2011 that figure was 97 million litres; in 1998, Eddie Stobart trucks travelled 88 million miles a year; in 2011 that figure was 180 million miles; and in 1998, Eddie Stobart owned four million square feet of warehouse space; in 2011 that figure was nearly seven million square feet.

Such startling growth and success were inevitably recognised by the firm's peers. In 2011 the company won the prestigious 'Logistics Safety Award' as well as numerous other trophies for logistics and sustainable distribution achievements. Back in the summer of 2005, the independent Business Superbrands Council, made up of leading figures in the business and marketing world, voted Eddie Stobart into an extremely exclusive group of companies who hold the title of 'Business Superbrand'.

The annual announcement is complemented by a luxurious book, detailing the companies, which also included Sony, BT, JCB, Aston Martin, Dr. Martens and Shell, among others. Eddie Stobart has appeared in the list every year since and at the time of writing is placed at Number 15. With the business now a PLC, this brand profile has a significant impact on the actual value of the company.

In 2007, the Superbrands panel said: 'Eddie Stobart is a bold and powerful brand, despite an increasingly challenging and competitive market. The brand has ensured the personal touch and a sense of humour have not been lost despite its massive growth, for example the girls' names and punch graphics. More seriously it has heavily invested in technology... and has clearly shown how its core values of honesty, commitment and fast excellent services have all contributed to its success.'

BRANDING AND LOGO EVOLUTION

Among the many changes to the Eddie Stobart fleet since the hugely successful takeover in 2004, perhaps the most immediately striking was the complete redesign of the company livery. This coincided with the introduction of the vinyl wrapping of each truck (more of which later). 'We asked our designers to come up with a twenty-first century design,' said William at the time, but he was also keen for the new look to retain key features of the famous and iconic Stobart livery such as the cab arrows.

As these examples show, the original signwriting of the famous name was rather flowery, in keeping with the very ornate artwork painted onto many trucks by hand. In the early days, the brand's famous red arrow had yellow edging with a yellow 'S' inside; later there was a yellow 'S' inside a circular green badge, edged in a yellow rope design, with the initials E and P incorporated inside the curves of the 'S' (the rope circle is an ancient heraldic device, adapted by many traditional truck signwriters). A variety of monograms and typefaces were tried over the years, until eventually the arrow symbol and bold italic namestyle were established.

By the 1990s the arrow had been redesigned into a more modern-looking logo, still red with yellow, and there was also a period when it was gold on green. Yellow had previously been added to the red and green in the 1970s, but the modern fleet would soon just use red, green and white (there is now a paint colour called 'Eddie Stobart Green'). The famous red side-skirts came in around the mid-1990s.

For the 2005 revamp, the company changed the font used for the girls' names on the front of the trucks, so as to be much easier to read. The wording on the trucks also changed: standard Eddie Stobart trucks had previously carried a yellow-and-red shaded effect reading 'Eddie Stobart Ltd', with the strapline 'Express Road Haulage Specialist', although the strapline 'International Logistics' had also been used. The main identity changed to just 'Eddie Stobart' with white lettering and no shading effect, with the strapline 'Trans – Store – Logistics'.

They also added the name above the fleet number on the side of the vehicle, as well as a reflective Stobart arrow which was incorporated into the cabside design in place of the traditional crossed flags. The introduction of vinyl wrapping and computerised vinyl printing even made the modern Stobart arrow look 3D. The first vehicles to carry the new design were the 120 Volvo FH12 Globetrotter XLs which had recently joined the fleet. A further 50 DAF 95XF artics and 40 Scania Topline drawbars complemented them a few months later. Shortly after, Stobart added three distinctive blue lights fitted to each lower front grille.

The following year, the firm altered the trailer livery too. Gone was the block italic lettering which was replaced by the new Eddie Stobart logo in white with a red outline. There was also a redesigned skirt with red-and-white chevrons, replacing the traditional coachlines. The rear doors had a makeover with the new arrow design and logo overlaid in a high-visibility material. Notably the website address was also very prominent. An initial set of one hundred trailers were launched in April 2005, with a further two hundred following throughout the rest of the year. In addition, new white trailers were added to complement the more common green units, these having walking floors.

To coincide with this extensive rebranding, Stobart also revamped their famous uniform. February 2007 saw the launch of a brand new uniform intended to match the updated livery. Extensive trials with samples were undertaken by a number of drivers to weed out faults and design issues; William had said he wanted a 'sportier' look to the uniform, similar to that of the motorsport teams which the firm now sponsored. At the time of writing, new employees are issued with ten shirts, three or four pairs of trousers, boots, a belt and a branded fleece. //

The evolution of a brand:
Eddie Stobart Mercedes trucks -
1973 and 2012.

Beyond Trucking

A REMARKABLE RENAISSANCE THAT HAS SEEN STOBART EXPAND FROM A TRUCKING LEGEND INTO A LOGISTICS INNOVATOR, BEFORE EVOLVING ONCE AGAIN INTO A BRANDING PHENOMENON WITHIN SPORT, TELEVISION AND MODERN ENTERTAINMENT CULTURE.

After the purchase of the company back in 2004 by William Stobart and Andrew Tinkler, the cautious path would have been consolidation; regroup, restructure and cement the legacy of the name within the trucking business. However, that was clearly not the strategy favoured by the ever-ambitious childhood friends. How their shared proactive expansion ideology has manifested itself is startling: as well as moving the business into new logistics markets, they have developed an exciting programme of involvement within numerous high-level sports. Stobart is no longer just a logistics company – now it is a multi-layered modern branding phenomenon.

STOBART RAIL

Eddie Stobart first considered entering the railway market back in 1998, keen to take a share of a rail freight industry that is worth billions each year. There was an abortive attempt at running a luxury passenger train but the real prize was rail freight. The enormous set-up cost and logistical challenges of entering this market meant this was not a step to be taken lightly, but with Andrew Tinkler's massive success in that industry with his firm WA Developments, the company was finally able to launch Stobart Rail on 19 September 2006 (WA Developments was taken over by Eddie Stobart in April 2008).

The first locomotive, called simply Eddie The Engine, was a Class 66. These massive engines can pull 2200 tonnes – the same weight as 50 standard trucks – and can reach a speed of 75mph. Eddie (and later his younger sibling, Bart the Engine) was capable of hauling 26 specially designed, curtain-sided containers, 45-feet long and eight feet six inches high. The firm ordered 90 of these special containers from China for the launch of Stobart Rail, which was the first fully liveried dedicated freight train to go into operation in the UK. A huge contract with Tesco was the first load, taking goods from Daventry International Rail Freight Terminal to Tesco's colossal distribution centre in Livingston, Scotland (even with this railway assistance, 850 Stobart truck drivers can be working on a Tesco load at any one time!).

One of the prime concerns with launching the rail division was efficiency, and it's clear that the savings on fuel and emissions can be remarkable. Each year the rail division carries goods that reduce carbon emissions by 22,400 tonnes, which cuts total Stobart Group fuel usage by 20 per cent. One train-load of around 36 containers is the equivalent of 28 trucks in volume and can be taken over 700 miles in one day. The same amount of freight taken by lorries would need 19,600 road miles, which means the train reduces congestion effectively by almost 19,000 miles. Similarly, the lorries would need in excess of 11,000 litres of fuel

Above: *Stobart Rail has its own distinctive blue-and-while livery to distinguish it from its freight counterparts.*

per trip whereas the train only needs just over 3,000 litres. This represents an annual saving of over two million litres, great news for both the environment and the road congestion, and to be fair also for Eddie Stobart's coffers!

The introduction of the service replaced 13,000 lorry journeys per annum, equivalent to three million lorry miles or 180,000 tonnes being taken off the roads. This is the equivalent of the entire Eddie Stobart fleet being taken off the road for three weeks. The reduction in carbon emissions is dramatic.

The service relies heavily on the West Coat main line which unfortunately means that if there's an accident – as when a Virgin train crashed on 23 February 2007 – the trains are potentially stranded. However, Stobart had planned ahead and only bought railway stock and containers that could travel on any gauge railway line in the UK, thus enabling them to quickly re-route their trains with only a slight delay. Notably, after the above crash, Stobart sent their Motorsport hospitality tent to be constructed near the crash site to help feed and shelter the incident investigators, police, etc.

Stobart also run a service between Valencia and Barking, Essex. The seasonal rail service carries chilled containers of fruit and vegetables from Spain to supermarkets and retailers in the UK.

Stobart's rail freight division carries a smart blue-and-white livery so as to distinguish it from the haulage business. There are also five special rail division low-loader road vehicles, also in blue livery and (of course) complete with girls' names, which deliver equipment for contracted repair work. These 560bhp lorries are notably more powerful than the standard Stobart curtain-siders and are strong enough to pull eight double-decker buses weighing a total of 40 tonnes. Their hydraulic ramps allow easy loading and they can ingeniously be extended from eight to ten feet in width to carry unusually wide loads.

This division also has its own large maintenance team, who carry out over five hundred repairs every year. Stobart Rail offer rail network maintenance, repair and replacement including such services as earthworks, bridge replacement, drainage, track renewal, ground stabilising and emergency works. This requires many specialist and very expensive machines; although Andrew Tinkler was a universally acknowledged market-leading expert in this field, even his know-how cannot make the equipment come cheap! Take the Gopher – a huge beast designed to remove old ballast from under the railway lines without disturbing the existing tracks. This massive machine is seventeen tonnes in weight, 11.6 metres long and sits astride the railway lines. The giant vehicle cannot travel on public roads and has to be ferried to the site on a low-loader.

Once it is sitting on top of the tracks, 3.6-metre long arms scoop out the old ballast from under the track and push it into a 2.7-metre wheel, which in turn carries the stones up and onto a five-metre conveyor belt for removal. Once correctly positioned, the Gopher can remove two hundred tonnes of ballast in just twelve hours. There are currently only a handful of people able to teach how to drive and operate the Gopher. And the cost? Over £250,000 for each Gopher.

With Stobart Rail already recognised as a market innovator and highly respected player in the field, Eddie Stobart has grand designs to be the Number One domestic rail operator in the UK.

STAT//

STOBART DELIVERS SEVEN MILLION CANS OF ONE PARTICULARLY POPULAR COLA EACH WEEK.

STOBART AIR AND SOUTHEND AIRPORT

When Andrew Tinkler and William Stobart took over the firm in 2004, they were absolutely focused in their vision to create a so-called 'multi-modal' business, in other words one that offers the complete package of transport services, namely 'road, rail, sea and air'. Their official website heralds the idea of 'The future of multimodal logistics'.

In pursuit of this goal, in 2008, Eddie Stobart bought Southend Airport for £21 million. At the time, mostly private planes used the airport with a charter airline also operating there in the summer. However, William and Andrew Tinkler had much more ambitious plans.

Since the acquisition, the company has spent a further £78 million on state-of-the-art technology and a massive refurbishment including a complete overhaul of the terminal building, a new 26-metre control tower and new radar systems. A new train station was completed in 2010 to service the passengers in and out of London (it's only 50 minutes into the capital), runways have been extended and a larger workforce employed, including twenty-four full-time firemen. At the same time a 5 per cent stake in Aer Arran has been acquired with designs on turning Southend into a major passenger hub for access to London and the Southeast. The target is to see two million passengers a year passing through the doors of Southend Airport by 2020. With Easyjet opening a service there in 2011 and plans for a hotel in the pipeline, there is little doubt that Stobart will achieve its aim.

STOBART PORT

Container freight is massive business in the UK and each year more than seven million containers arrive at British ports. Over 300,000 go to Stobart's very own port in Widnes, the official title of which is Mersey Multimodal Gateway, also known as 3MG. This specialist container handling and port operation is part of the Stobart O'Connor

division following the acquisition of O'Connor in 2008; previously these vehicles had a different blue livery but all now carry the standard Stobart company livery, with the name O'Connor on the red-and-green trucks' tractor unit.

This inland port's most vital links to the commercial centres of Britain are by rail. The freight trains that serve it sometimes stretch to over half a mile in length and weigh over 1,400 tonnes, but nevertheless Widnes is capable of handling 14 of them a day, all rammed with containers weighing up to 35 tonnes each. To receive this huge volume of goods, the port can work with over 1,000 trucks a day and over 16,000 containers can be stored there for later dispatch. Each year, the port brings in goods from more than one hundred countries.

Known as 'boxes' in the trade, these containers are lifted on one of four gantry cranes, which are six storeys high and can move around 800 boxes a day. As the waiting trucks queue for their pick-ups, the four cranes work tirelessly to unload the massive trains, using a giant claw known as a spreader. Each crane has a GPS system inside which tells the driver where each box is and where it needs to go, a pairing verified by matching the box number and the vehicle registration.

Above: *Stobart is proud to service British armed forces stationed in Europe.*

STOBART INTERNATIONAL

In 1999, Eddie Stobart launched its international division, making trips to Europe and occasionally further afield (the furthest from base that a Stobart truck ever made it was Kosovo). The company had worked across Europe sporadically before; the very first venture across the water came way back in January 1990, when a truck driven by a man coincidentally named William Stobbart (no relation and a different spelling of his surname) took a load to Frankfurt and then backloaded some goods to the Midlands in his Euro-Drag drawbar.

However, 1999 was when the company launched a major push into Europe, at a time when the single currency was looking to unite and empower business on the continent. While the UK's so-called trampers are a special breed, staying in their trucks from Monday to Friday, the international tramper is an even rarer beast, sometimes staying away for twelve weeks at a time! There are 80 international trampers who notch up 5,000 trips each year.

One of the company's regular European routes is to drop supplies off to NAAFI stores, the supermarkets that supply British goods to UK armed forces abroad. Given the high proportion of truckers who are either ex-armed forces or have parents who were in the army, this seems a particularly appropriate contract. In fact, a notable percentage of Stobart drivers are ex-Forces. This close relationship was cemented during the 1990s Kosovo crisis, when Eddie Stobart trucks delivered supplies to British forces based in neighbouring Macedonia.

With Stobart's Irish division opening two years earlier in 2008 with a brand new base in Dublin, 175 staff and 150 more trucks bedecked in special Irish livery, the famous and iconic vehicles now seem to have made themselves a permanent feature across most of Europe! A Stobart truck will make a delivery every 20 seconds somewhere on the continent.

STOBART ON TV

The Eddie Spotters are an army of fans that see the famous trucks as genuine celebrities. This phenomenon was fuelled hugely in 2010 during Stobart's 40th anniversary year when the revered Princess Productions TV company, along with Channel 5, filmed a television series dedicated to the famous haulage firm, called *Trucks & Trailers*. The first series of six episodes was broadcast in September 2010 and scored instantly strong ratings, sometimes as high as two million viewers. This wasn't the first time TV stations had taken an interest in Stobart: back in 1990, Border Television took a film crew out with a truck along the M6, as well as interviewing Edward and filming footage of the Carlisle depot, all for the magazine

Above: Trucks & Truckers *became one of Channel 5's biggest ratings hits.*

show *Lookaround*. Previously, company secretary Barrie Thomas had been seen on screen awarding a cheque to local business winners of Enterprise Challenge. Also, in 1999, a video called *The Story of Eddie Stobart* was sold through WH Smith and was that chain's biggest selling VHS in the leisure genre.

So the media's fascination with Eddie Stobart was nothing new. However, *Trucks & Trailers* was easily the biggest and best TV coverage yet. To date, two further series have followed, turning the drivers and Stobart employees who appear on screen into celebrities. Each series takes around ten weeks to film and sees drivers shadowed by a film crew. Later in this book, you will meet my driver companions – Mark Dixon, Tim Fox and Fiona Soltysiak – who are all regulars on the TV show.

Above: *Fiona was an obvious candidate for* Trucks & Trailers.

Fiona was an obvious candidate for the TV crew of *Trucks & Trailers* to follow, because she is an exception and also because she is so positive and buoyant. It's probably this optimism that has strengthened her resolve during the harder days at work when people are narrow-minded towards her.

'The first time the TV crew followed me it was nerve-wracking. We had to learn how to answer the question in a way that worked on TV, it was interesting to learn. You have to ignore the camera but it's hard at first because it's big and it's constantly on you! But we all learned, and ultimately I just need to do my job, which takes the pressure off. By the second series, I was far more settled and we just cracked on. It's certainly different and more than anything it was nice for me to have someone in the cab to chat to, otherwise you do go a bit crazy spending so long on your own, especially on nights when you can't phone anybody.

'It is kind of weird when people recognise me in the street, it's certainly not what I expected when I started driving trucks. The oddest part is when other drivers tell me stuff about myself when they have never met me before. No one's been horrible to me and it's all good fun, I've generally just had really nice comments. And at the end of the day we are all just truck drivers.

'When Channel 5 is following us around,' continues Fiona, 'it's more entertaining of course. The depots where we are going know in advance that it's being filmed and it does make people more interested. I seem to be able to shut that out and get on with my job.'

Tim Fox has really enjoyed the filming despite it sometimes making his day a little more protracted: 'It makes a bit of a difference, it slows you down a bit but we still get the work done. We make allowances for it, so we set out earlier or whatever. They are all genuine jobs too that we take them on, it's not staged for TV. And people seem to like the fat lad from up north!'

Perhaps his recent taste of fame on the TV show has distracted him from the trucking life? 'You're not a celebrity, you're not even famous, you're a truck driver, that's what pays the wages. Everyone likes to be liked, the TV show did make me feel nice, I'm not going to lie, and it was fun to do, but at the end of the day I'm a truck driver, always have been, probably always will be.'

For Mark Dixon, *Trucks & Trailers* has been something he has enjoyed doing too, but he hasn't forgotten his roots: 'Monday to Friday I'll be driving but every now and then I get a phone call asking me to park up suddenly and get a train to London for something to do with the TV. Before the first series started there were notices going up on boards around Stobart saying, "Do you want to be on TV?" I didn't even put my name down, didn't bat an eyelid. But then I was in Birmingham one day and I got a phone call and they said, "Mark, where are you now? Turn round now and go to Appleton." I was like, "What have I done wrong? That's where all the big managers are!" When I got there, the Channel 5 producers were there, so I spoke to them and decided to give it a go. They seemed to like what they filmed with me.' Mark has become something of a Stobart celebrity and has over 19,000 followers on Twitter. His mobile phone is constantly pinging with messages as his fans enjoy staying in touch. 'You see the TV show making me out to be a celebrity but I'm not, I'm just a lorry driver.'

Above: *Mark Dixon is now one of the firm's most famous drivers.*

STOBART AND SPORT

Although Eddie Stobart never advertises conventionally, it has over the years sponsored a number of sports teams that all bring the company a huge amount of profile. The first sport to carry the famous trucking name was football, when the firm decided to sponsor Carlisle United FC back in 1995. This team have never been the very best in the UK but even when they came bottom of the third division of the Football League, Stobart did not abandon them – consequently the company can currently claim to be the longest-serving sponsor of a football team in the UK. William believes this partnership is for the benefit of the whole of Carlisle, not necessarily just for his business.

Another area where Stobart is very prominent is rally and motorsport. As a kid Edward was a huge fan of Stirling Moss, and both Andrew Tinkler and William were also massive rally fans as youngsters. The Stobart Motorsport division started in 2004 when Stobart joined forces with the M Sport team run by Malcolm Wilson. They first took part in the 2004 Kwik Fit Pirelli British Championship, with a brace of Ford Focus rally cars built by M Sport. Owner Malcolm was a multiple rally champion and his son Matthew was one of Stobart's rally drivers. The decision was a personal one at first – both William Stobart and Andrew Tinkler had bought rally cars in their early twenties and were keen followers of the sport. However, they have both been very pleased by the subsequent business benefit.

Like all sectors of the business, Stobart Motorsport always aim to maintain the highest standards of performance – in recognition of this it was named 'Rally Business of the Year' at the prestigious Motorsport Industry Association Awards in 2008.

'Andrew was more into rallying than I was,' explains William openly. 'We started sponsoring Malcolm Wilson's rally team, it was a good deal at the time, it got us on the bigger stage, and it got us recognition around Europe and the world. We've actually gained a lot of contracts through that link-up, for example

STAT//

DURING THE BUSY FESTIVE PERIOD, STOBART TRUCKS DELIVER OVER 375,000 CHRISTMAS TREES.

Opposite: *Stobart launched their motorsport division in 2004.*

WORLD RALLY DOUBLE-DECKER MEGA TRAILER

This Scania has an impressive 500bhp, V8 engine with a pulling power of 40 tonnes. Inside its cavernous trailer it can carry three hundred wheels, 20 bumpers, 60 car panels and various other paraphernalia needed for the World Rally team, such as the marquee and service park for the cars themselves. It carries its own 'piggy-back' forklift on the back and has smaller wheels than a normal truck, to lower the ride height in order to fit underneath smaller European bridges. With each rally car worth around £250,000, it's pretty vital that the trucks don't crash!

we did all the haulage for the Ford World rally team, we do Pirelli tyres and at every Formula One GP in Europe we will have 40 vehicles working. That's all via the motorsport. And we've also met a lot of very talented people through that sponsorship who are now part of our management team.' Notably, as well as ex-motorsport people, many members of the Stobart management team are also ex-truck drivers who, like William and Edward before them, have worked their way up through the ranks.

Above: *One of the company's most prestigious contracts is working with the Mercedes Petronas Formula 1 team.*

William proudly mentions the company's involvement in Formula One, most obviously their contract with Mercedes Petronas F1, home to Nico Rosberg and the seven-time world champion Michael Schumacher. This wasn't the first time they had worked with a Formula One team – in 2004 the Minardi Formula One team needed to get eight replica cars flown out to South Africa as part of a fund-raising programme for Nelson Mandela's Children's Fund, so Stobart dived in to help. The cars were placed in specially constructed wooden transport boxes and taken from the Minardi HQ in Ledbury to Bournemouth International Airport for the flight to South Africa.

So when the opportunity to drive the Mercedes Petronas cars from their base in Brackley to all the European F1 races came up for tender, Eddie Stobart was perfectly placed to secure this highly prestigious contract. Stobart are not allowed to use their own livery on the trucks that carry the actual race cars – these are painted in the Mercedes Petronas colours as they will be highly visible on race weekend. The eight-man team don't wear Eddie Stobart uniforms either, again donning the Mercedes Petronas clothing. The actual race cars are shipped in custom-made

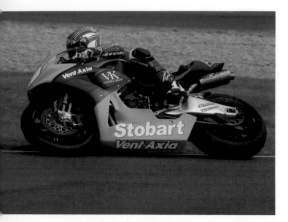

Above: *Sponsoring various strands of motorsport has yielded many productive business links for Stobart.*

trucks such as the RT4, each of which has two floors, with the spare engines, gearboxes and other parts sitting on the bottom layer, while the all-important cars are situated safely on the top deck. These trucks cost around £200,000 each but when they are filled with two Formula One cars and all the equipment the value rockets to over an incredible £7 million! The £3 million cars are each fitted with old tyres during transit then strapped to the top deck with the utmost caution – no 'tip and run' here! There is also a £1 million so-called 'Treehouse Trailer' that becomes the Mercedes offices when *in situ* at the races. These precious cargoes are followed by three more trucks in standard Stobart livery carrying all the support equipment. Even though the loaded truck with the race cars on board is worth so much money, it still covers nearly 90,000 miles per season.

In 2005 Stobart added a superbike team to the motorsport division. Having won the British championship in 1999 under the Vimto Honda banner, the team – led by Cumbrian businessman Paul Bird – repeated their success in later years using the Stobart-branded Honda Fireblades. The team has been one of the most successful teams in the recent history of the British Superbike Championship.

For Stobart truck drivers, being part of the motorsport division is very prestigious. Whenever Stobart advertise for new drivers they are swamped with applications even though the hours are very long and each driver also has to work on many different disciplines. For example, once the rally-team truckers have driven the cars to the race, they must then not only disembark the cars but also unload and then build the marquee for corporate hospitality (where the staff will typically serve nine hundred meals per race), as well as construct the service area for the rally cars themselves. When Stobart won the contract to deliver all Pirelli tyres to the European F1 circuit, the firm had to recruit a team of ten expert drivers; over 150 drivers applied, even though the job will require stints of up to six weeks away from home at a time and only a very slim chance of ever seeing a race car!

Another sport that Stobart is heavily involved in is Rugby League. For 2012, the company sponsored the top flight of the game under the banner 'Stobart Super League'. Each of the 14 teams have a number of dedicated trailers (there are more than 100 Super League trailers in total) with gigantic photos of some of their players on the side, a real treat for the Spotters! Also there is a one-off trailer featuring a group photograph of all the captains, making a very rare 'post' for fans of the brand.

Given Eddie Stobart's decision to buy an unbroken horse and train it for horse and cart work way back in the 1940s, it is intriguing that the modern Stobart company has an active involvement in polo. It's fairly symbolic of just how far that the agricultural contracting firm has come that today it is an active participant in what is known as 'the sport of kings'.

The connection started when Stobart bought a rival haulage firm called James Irlams, who already had a polo team. Then, in a match against the Sultan of Brunei's team, the Southeast Asian monarch was so impressed with the Stobart operation at the event that he contracted the company to transport all his horses around Europe on the polo circuit. Stobart is also an official sponsor of the Cheshire Polo Club, and William's son Edward is a member of the team too (he is also a qualified HGV Class 1 LGV C+E driver).

As with all things Eddie Stobart, only the best will do and this applies more than ever for a sport that is so prestigious. Consequently the company bought one of the world's biggest horseboxes to work with the polo team, decked out in the unique Stobart polo team livery. This climate-controlled vehicle can carry 18 horses in a luxury trailer, with two CCTV cameras filming the valuable animals' every move to make sure they are safe. There are separate bays for each horse, and also eight large storage compartments for the necessary equipment. The truck's suspension is of exceptional quality as this helps reduce the shock to the horses' fragile legs while in transit.

STAT//

IN 2007, AS PART OF THE WHITEHAVEN MARITIME FESTIVAL, TWENTY STOBART TRUCKS DROVE IN CONVOY FROM CARLISLE AIRPORT TO WHITEHAVEN HARBOUR, WITH WILLIAM STOBART AT THE WHEEL OF THE LEADING TRUCK. THEY WERE DELIVERING A CONTAINER WRAPPED AS A PRESENT, WHICH CONTAINED A BOAT FOR THE WHITEHAVEN SEA CADETS AS A THANK-YOU FOR THEIR WORK FOR THE TOWN.

There are also four further dedicated horse trucks in the fleet used to service the polo team, each one costing around £120,000. These more standard vehicles are capable of carrying ten horses at a time in a safe, secure and climate-controlled environment. Each truck also has a galley kitchen, a shower room and a toilet. When the truck arrives at its location, the side has a pull-out canopy for entertaining.

As with fuel-tanker drivers, extra special attention has to be paid to driving these trucks. Harsh braking and reckless acceleration can frighten the horses and potholes can cause potentially life-threatening injuries. If a horse starts panicking and injures a leg through kicking the sides of the lorry, there is a possibility that the animal will have to be put down.

It's not just the polo team that has horses. Stobart CEO Andrew Tinkler is a horse breeder with over 20 years' experience who owns more than 70 thoroughbreds. His steeds are often raced all around the world, and given that the horses could each cost as much as £20,000 (sometimes more), their safe and healthy transportation is essential.

Andrew's trailer is even more high-tech, costing £430,000. This air-conditioned Oakley horse box carries just five of his precious horses at once and its inside is absolutely exquisite, with hand-stitched leather upholstery and even an on-board 'horse sauna'. This is clearly not a cheap hobby – when the horses were sent to race in the Dubai Carnival, for example, each one racked up a £7,000 bill just for the return flight. //

TELLYTUBBY TRUCK

One of the more dramatic Eddie Stobart vehicles is the so-called 'Tellytubby' lorry (F1494). This is a £300,000, 25-tonne, one-off vehicle that carries inside a state-of-the-art, 27-metre LED screen. This is used for sponsored and corporate events and offers the chance to park the lorry at a site and then erect this huge screen for the public to watch.

Once parked up, what appears to be a regular rigid Volvo truck quickly transforms at the switch of a button: massive hydraulic rams push a gigantic screen vertically into place, while inside a production and editing suite enables experts to capture and edit footage from the day's events. One use which viewers of the TV show will recognise is filming and supporting the annual Gumball Rally, where a variety of supercars are driven across parts of Europe. For this event, footage of the race is filmed and then edited, and provided that the Tellytubby arrives at the next stage in time – it can only travel at 56mph, which is rather slower than the supercars! – it can then show the clips of that very same day.

Part Two/

Eddie Stobart on the Road

A Day
in the Life

A FIRST-HAND ACCOUNT OF A DROP IN AN EDDIE STOBART
LORRY: 'A STATIONARY TRUCK MAKES NO MONEY.'

All those years of entrepreneurial success and unquenchable hard work were foremost in my mind when on a bright winter's day in early 2012 I drove up to Carlisle, the spiritual home of the modern-day Eddie Stobart company. I'd asked to drive an Eddie Stobart lorry and also spend time with various drivers making deliveries, so that I could experience their life first-hand. My contact at the company, special projects manager Laura Tinkler, had arranged these events with military precision and speedy efficiency, so within a few short days of making the request I was heading north to experience life as an Eddie Stobart driver.

As I passed Manchester and headed up the northerly stretches of the M6, the stunning vistas of the Lake District framed the road, looming large over the streaming traffic. When my sat-nav told me that Carlisle approached, I could see several minuscule dwellings on the hillsides, and as I did I cast my mind back to the Stobart family farm where it had all started. Forty years after the company had first been incorporated, the family business has gone from being a small local concern led by Eddie, then on to a market-leading haulier inspired by his son Edward, and finally, with William Stobart and his best friend Andrew Tinkler at the helm since 2004, it has evolved into a multi-modal logistics company turning over more than half a billion pounds each year.

The famous Carlisle depot of Eddie Stobart is a hub of relentless activity; everywhere you look there are red and green trucks passing by, drivers scurrying around and trailers being loaded by forklifts that nip in and out of cavernous warehouses. Everything is soundtracked by the hissing of air-brakes and the clunking of pallets on trailer floors. Stobart have bigger and far more modern depots around the country, but this is where it all began. Every day, more than two hundred trucks drive in and out of this depot which is spread-eagled across one corner of a local industrial estate. At any given moment, there might be 140 million empty tins stored here.

I was due to go on a drop with Mark Dixon, one of Stobart's best-known drivers. As expected, he was bang on time, having arrived at the depot earlier that morning ahead of schedule. He walked over and held out his hand with a smile, and I immediately noticed his immaculate Stobart uniform, crisp and spotless, with not a seam or stitch out of place.

We were due to pick up some metal coils from a warehouse nearby and then deliver them to a canning factory about half-an-hour away. First off Mark gave me a high-visibility jacket and then led the way across to his truck, Phoebe Grace, which is named after his daughter. His very first Stobart truck had been called

Gabrielle Rose after his other daughter (Stobart drivers used to get first refusal on the truck's names, but this started to cause problems when they fell out with wives or girlfriends!).

As with Mark himself, the first thing I noticed about Phoebe Grace was her immaculate presentation. The paintwork on Mark's Volvo truck was so gleaming it was almost blinding in the early morning sun. As a so-called 'tramper', Mark lives and sleeps in his truck from Monday to Friday, only returning home at weekends. As with most trampers he will often drive over five hundred miles a day, so this is not so much a vehicle of work but his second home. As he walked alongside, he spotted a speck of dirt on the bumper and began wiping it off with a small cloth, frowning until the blemish was removed, then a smile returned to his face.

He opened the passenger door for me and my first impression was just how incredibly high the cabin was. Four metal grated steps climbed up to the seat with a long vertical handle to the left-hand side to help haul yourself up. It was steep and quite a pull as I clumsily climbed up, but when I did so the heavy door started to close on me, so I had to perch precariously with one hand pushing the door back while I completed the climb; I looked across only to find Mark was already in his seat and pulling his seat belt across.

The cabin was spotlessly clean. There were several signs of the 'home-from-home' nature of this truck scattered around, such as a teddy bear, a couple of kids' toys, Mark's glasses, a shaver and a flask. Mark showed me around the inside of his cab with the same pride as if we were strolling around a swanky apartment. There was a six-feet six-inch bed tucked tightly behind the two seats, with a noticeably narrow mattress. There was a storage net swinging above the mattress (a tramper's wardrobe as it were), and underneath the bed was a fridge. A coffee-maker can be stowed above the dash, and he also had a Freeview TV and even a smoke alarm. The ceiling of the cab was surprisingly high, enough for most men to almost stand up straight in, which is just as well given the huge amount of time the drivers spend

STAT//

850 STOBART DRIVERS CAN BE WORKING ON A TESCO CONTRACT AT ANY ONE TIME.

A Stobart driver's cab has many of the modern luxuries that you would usually expect to find in a 'home-from-home'. In this Volvo FH XL globetrotter, a driver is seen using his hand-held GTS device to update the Stobart's planning department on his whereabouts.

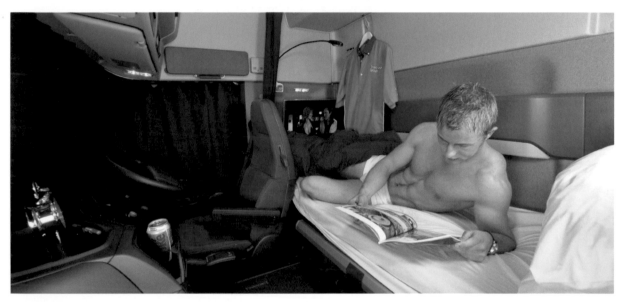

in their trucks. A wrap-around curtain was attached around the upper reaches of the cab's interior for privacy.

Mark's truck is the home of a tramper and is therefore different to those used by the army of day and night drivers. The vehicles themselves are identical, on paper, but day drivers are usually given a different lorry each day – their vehicles are much more tools to use to complete a job. Both trampers and day/night drivers, however, have to perform a series of regular safety checks, monitoring such items as coolant, tyre pressure and the correct functioning of all light and oil levels.

Every truck in the Stobart fleet is fitted with an Isotrack, a state-of-the-art GPS system that can track and trace the whereabouts, performance, load details and schedule of each lorry. When this system was first introduced, many drivers objected, feeling that they were being spied on, especially as the word 'freedom' is one that you hear very often when talking to Stobart trampers about why they love their job.

However, they quickly became accustomed to the Isotrack and it's more likely to be traffic jams than the GPS tracking system that causes grumbles among the drivers. The Isotrack feeds information back to base, where every truck is represented on a huge screen by either a green dot (loaded) or a red dot (empty). A red dot costs Eddie Stobart £1.50 per mile in fuel and wages. Edward was once quoted saying, 'The secret is never to have an empty truck. If you take lemonade down somewhere, bring water back up.'

Alongside all the electronics connecting the lorry with the office, there is also a panic button in case the driver feels his health or safety is at risk, or that his load is under threat. This button instantly alerts the planners who would in turn immediately contact the police for assistance.

The trucks don't have any washing or toilet facilities (yet), so the drivers have to rely on either Stobart-owned depots which are serviced regularly or the general public's truck-stop facilities which can often resemble a war zone of filth.

We pulled out of the depot and headed out onto the open road, chatting as we drove. Mark has been driving trucks since 2002 and working for Eddie Stobart since 2006. Previously he started his working life as a carpet-fitter but he always had his eye on driving for a living and aged 22 he did just that: 'I trained up and eventually passed as a qualified carpet-fitter but when I went to the boss and asked to be paid the same as the established workers, he gave me my P45! I'd been driving their works vans so I went from that to being a white van man for about four years. Then I just bored of that and thought, I want to do my HGV.

'I wanted something different, I was just a van driver and I'd see lorries and think, I want to do that now. So I did my Class 2, paid for that myself, then worked for a firm who helped me train some more; within six months I had my Class 1. Stobart was down the road from where I lived and I knew it was a big firm but I didn't know anything about the "brand" until I started working for them.'

We quickly arrived at the collection point, a set of warehouses secreted away at the end of a housing estate that seemed to have impossibly narrow roads and sharp turns. My slight agitation that we would get stuck in this massive truck was entirely down to my inexperience rather than Mark's driving, as he calmly flowed through the smallest of streets with ease. 'Mind you, we have had drivers shot at with air rifles along this stretch,' he said, at which I leaned back in my seat and slumped down away from the window perhaps a little more than necessary.

We pulled up at the warehouse into a welcomingly open car park – already I'd begun to view the world through a trucker's eyes: how wide are the entrances, where are the loading bays, are there any vehicles in the way? Obstacles that you wouldn't even notice in a car were now make-or-break difficulties to get past. Thankfully this was a simple start to the day so Mark easily parked up and we headed into the office to collect the paperwork.

Then it was back out into the yard where Mark began opening up the curtain-side trailer, which he did by releasing a series of ratchet tie-down straps, known as 'curtain clips'. He then walked to the back of the trailer and started hauling the heavy curtain towards him, reeling it in and exposing the empty shell of the trailer. He then removed the vertical metal columns that run along the length of the trailer, and when this was complete, he signalled for the waiting fork-lift that he was ready to receive the load.

Right on schedule, a fairly sizeable fork-lift truck chugged out of the darkness of its warehouse home carrying the first of several huge metal coils. Each one of the larger coils weighed approximately ten tonnes and had come all the way from South Africa. Each coil was worth around £30,000 and contained thousands of linear metres of coil. Stobart's part in the process was to take these coils to a canning factory nearby, where they would be turned into cans for beer and fizzy drinks.

The coils were loaded quickly and without incident but then Mark had to secure them, a task which was particularly vital as heavy coils like this had been known to fall sideways off trucks if poorly fastened. If one of these coils slipped off the trailer, it would effectively be the same as five Range Rovers falling off the lorry at once.

Fully loaded, the coils had added 24 tonnes of weight to the sixteen-and-a-half tonne truck (cab unit and empty trailer). At many bigger drops there are weighbridges, but if not then the paperwork calculating the total weight has to be checked and double-checked by more than one person. To help the precision loading, many trucks are fitted with a pressure gauge at the rear to ascertain if the trailer is overloaded.

The maximum legally allowed capacity is 44 tonnes; clearly, if more goods are squeezed on than this weight limit allows, then a haulier could in theory make more money. However, to deter those tempted to break the law there are very strict penalties: exceeding his load could land Mark with a £200 personal fine and a £5000 penalty for Stobart.

STAT//

IN 2011 EDDIE STOBART ENTERED THREE TRUCKS INTO THE ANNUAL 'REAR OF THE YEAR' COMPETITION! THE TRAILERS' REAR DOORS WERE EMBLAZONED WITH, 'THE ONLY WAY IS AMY'; 'HER ROYAL HOTNESS' AND 'DOES MY BUMPER LOOK BIG, PET?' SADLY, THEY DID NOT WIN THE COVETED TROPHY.

Mark Dixon has been a tramper for Stobart since 2006. He lives on the road five days every week and covers in excess of 100,000 miles a year.

Once the load was safely secured, Mark pulled the heavy curtain back into place and then reversed the process by fixing the curtain clips back into position. After signing the paperwork, we were off to the next stop to 'tip' our load. As we headed off, I asked Mark about his itinerant lifestyle: 'I'm a tramper, I'm out all week. I tried giving it up seven years ago, I thought, I should get back to a normal life and go home every day, but within six weeks I was back on the road again. I know I haven't got a normal life, because I'm away from family and friends all week. So I have to cram everything into two days, come the weekend I've got the kids, me mates… but sometimes even now I think, I just want to be normal for a change, but then if I have a week off work and I'm not going nowhere, I'm sat at home bored. I'm used to my own little bubble. It is solitary, yes. If you have small local drops you might get to know people but at the massive depots for the big clients you often don't recognise anyone.

'There's pros and cons. Come summer time I have got the best job in the world, while you lot are all sat in your offices, I'm sat here with the air-con on in the countryside, I can pull up for me break and sit in the open; obviously come winter time you are all sat in nice warm offices and I'm pulling curtains back covered in road salt, so then it's not so glamorous!

'Lorry drivers do a lot of thinking, sat here. I do wonder sometimes why I like being a tramper so much. Me dad was in the Forces, so I've lived in Germany, everywhere really. We would live somewhere for a year, if that, then move on and go somewhere else. So I was living in boxes all the time. Kinda like I am now, I suppose.

'At eight years old I was at boarding school, then we moved again when I was eleven. Back then I wanted to follow in me dad's footsteps and be a mechanic in the army. I used to go to work with him at a weekend and play around in all the tanks! But to be honest, if someone had said, "What do you want to be when you grow up?" I never ever would have said, "I want to be a lorry driver." I've always

//STAT

been a bit of a petrolhead, I love motorsports. I can't run, I can't swim but I love anything that takes petrol. But no, it wasn't my childhood dream to be a diesel gypsy.'

As we chatted, it was very noticeable how much more cumbersome the truck was with the full payload on the trailer. It was slower to pull away and its movements were more deliberate as it swayed under the considerable weight of its cargo. As we approached the drop-off, it was immediately clear this was not going to be as easy as the collection. The warehouse was in a complex of small, narrow service roads, with several trucks already waiting and the security barrier and lodge inconveniently wedged between two large buildings. Mark parked his truck and went off to get the paperwork while I stayed in the cabin and surveyed the proceedings; a maelstrom of trucks, drivers, fork-lifts and vans whizzing around, picking up, dropping off, delivering goods that keep the country moving. It almost felt like a secret world, as if I was part of some hidden population of Britain's behind-the-scenes workers.

I joined Mark at the lodge as he was just working out where to park; cleverly he'd looked on the site's CCTV for the best place to offload, but quite how he remembered the way to get through the maze-like site and park there once we were back in the cab I don't know. Mark parked expertly and the fork-lift removed the coils within a few minutes. With the curtain pulled back in place and the clips fixed back yet again, we were good to go. I noticed that Mark tucked the bottom of the curtain clip straps up inside themselves, and when I asked him why he explained that William insists on this as he dislikes seeing a Stobart truck driving along the road with the excess straps flapping about in the wind.

Already my time in the Stobart truck was beginning to make me re-evaluate several preconceptions. For starters, I'll never moan about the price of a fizzy drink again! I'd been on the collection, the journey to the drop-off, the delivery at the coil processing factory, then seen other trucks branded with soft drinks logos

Stobart lorries are carrying millions of cans of
fizzy drinks at any given minute.

pick up pallets full of empty cans to head off to the factory where the fizzy drinks would be poured into the shiny metal canisters. Then I could imagine these same cans being picked up again (probably by a Stobart truck, too) and heading off to a supermarket, only to be unloaded and unpacked once more, then finally placed by hand on to the shelves. And then I could see myself strolling into that supermarket and picking up that can of pop and thinking, 50p? Seems a bit steep.

Mark climbed back into his cab and we started our return journey back to the Carlisle depot. 'I remember starting tramping and doing my first ever night out, it was parked in a lay-by, first time I'd ever slept in a lay-by, I'd got no TV, nothing. I parked there, switched the engine off and thought, What the hell am I doing?! People are sat at home or in beer gardens having a pint and I'm sat in a lay-by. There was another lorry the other side of me, but his curtains were pulled shut, it was just a bizarre feeling. Being absolutely honest, it was quite scary at first, I was worrying about the security of the load, it's such a weird environment when you are not used to it. Of course, all these years later I'm just not bothered, wherever I run out of time I just park up and go to sleep, I don't give it a second thought!

'You still have to think about the load though. You try to work it out with the planners so you get your delivery off and then park up, empty. Obviously when you are doing distance work you sometimes have no choice but to park up with valuable goods on, but then you keep your wits about you and park up somewhere safe… nowhere's safe but if you park in the middle of a city with a curtain-side then you are probably going to wake up in the morning with no load! You kinda learn the safe routes and where to park.

'My trailer being a curtain-sider, someone can just get a knife and hack it. They ain't bothered what's in there, they will damage property to get in there and have a look. I never park in services normally because that's where all the lorry thieves operate, but one night I had no choice so I secured the lorry and went to the hotel. I woke up in the morning and there was a massive slash in me curtain. My trailer had two pallets on the back full of vitamin tablets; they weren't interested in that, but the damage was done. That can happen.'

It's not always the security of the load that is the worry. As Mark had mentioned earlier, some drivers were once shot at with airguns and, worse still, one unfortunate Stobart driver was held against his will while his load was stolen. Luckily, such extreme incidents are rare.

At other times, it is what tries to get in the truck rather than what people try to take out that troubles drivers. 'Once I parked in London to go into a soft drinks factory, dropped me trailer off and then picked one up that was already loaded and drove off. I went back to the same factory a few days later and they said, "Mark, you caused uproar last week!" It turned out the trailer I'd dropped off had someone hanging on underneath it, wrongly thinking I was going abroad. The police were called! How on earth they hang on under there I don't know; rather them than me.'

To an outsider, the legendary tales of a 'Drivers' Code' and the camaraderie of the open motorway carry a certain allure. Rather sadly, these are things that Mark thinks are in short supply. 'There used to be that community spirit. Drivers used to get on with other drivers. Now that seems to have gone and it's firms against firms, I will talk to anyone me, but some lorry drivers will think, You've just pinched our

STAT//

JUST EIGHT STOBART TRUCKS COULD DELIVER ONE MILLION CANS OF SOFT DRINK.

//STAT

DESPITE THE FAME OF THE STOBART SURNAME, MOST PEOPLE STILL EFFECTIVELY MISPRONOUNCE THE FAMILY MONIKER. POSSIBLY DERIVED FROM AN ANCIENT SCOTTISH WORD FOR POST OR STUMP, 'STOB', IN CONVERSATION WILLIAM PRONOUNCES IT 'STO-BUT' RATHER THAN 'STOW-BART'.

contract. It's kinda that atmosphere now, you used to park of a night time and get out and all the drivers would have a laugh. Not no more, they park next to you, shut their curtains and that's that.'

Ever the optimist, Mark thinks that the desperate financial times brought on by the credit crunch are partly to blame for this lack of community: 'I believe that spirit will eventually come back. People are stuck for money and if you park up and shut your curtains then you are not spending any money. Hopefully that will change.'

Trampers are famous for working long, demanding hours. On average they drive around 2500 miles a week, and usually around 100,000 miles a year. Most are paid by the hour: 'I often work 70 hours a week, including what they term a "period of availability" when you are not actually driving. We do some long hours, for sure. I enjoy that. To an outsider, tacho [tachograph – the device fitted to all trucks by law that records their mileage and hours spent driving] law is really confusing. We are allowed to do 48 hours a week. When we are sat loading it's not classed as work, yet when I open my curtains that's classed as work; when I'm driving it's classed as work, when I'm sat waiting I'm available for work but I can't do any, so it can get a little confusing. But one thing that is crystal-clear is that I'm away all week, so I don't want to park up early and not get paid for it. If I'm not going home, I might as well earn as much as I possibly can.'

There is an inherent risk in driving long hours in a lorry that weighs as much as 40 family cars, even with the four-and-a-half-hour time limit between breaks. 'I don't care what any driver says, if they are being honest every one of us has had that feeling when you are proper knackered and you have just got to pull over. In fact, not that many drivers will actually do the four and a half hours all the time. Back in the day, before I worked on trucks, I'd heard mates tell me how some bosses used to question why their drivers had had a break if they hadn't yet driven four-and-a-half hours, but now the whole industry is very safety-conscious. Stobart are very particular; they will even phone you up and say, "Mark, have yourself a break, half-an-hour". I would rather ring my boss up and say, "I'm half-an-hour late," than phone up and say, "Your truck's in a field 'cos I fell asleep behind the wheel." Stobart are really good, credit where credit's due. They will do everything they can and they do it right without breaking the law, they do everything by the book. They know that if a driver's tired then he needs to stop. The industry's days of fiddling tachos and stuff are gone now. Of course there are still some haulage firms… well… let's just say there are still people who know ways around things… but never Stobart. We do things correctly.' Eddie Stobart would be culpable for any accidents if its drivers did not take the correct breaks. For those who don't 'do things correctly', there is a £300 fine and a maximum penalty of jail time.

These strict standards also apply to getting the job in the first place: 'Back in the day it was a little bit more like, "Do you want a job? Yes? There's your keys, there's your truck, it's loaded, off you go!" You had a little driving assessment where you basically drove down the road, turned around and that was it. But now it's very different, there are so many tests and exams and regulations. Stobart run things with military precision.'

As we are driving along, an impatient car cuts up Mark's truck after an over-taking manoeuvre but despite uttering some choice words, he does so with a smile on his face and a laid-back sense of inevitability. This brings me to thinking of the dangers of being a truck driver, so I ask him if he's ever had an accident.

'I've had the odd bump but nothing exciting. Before I worked for Stobart, I was somewhere in London and I got stuck down this street all because one car was parked illegally, sat on double yellow lines on a bend to an industrial estate. I was there that long it caused a massive traffic jam so the police turned up. Basically they told me to do what I had to do to get out, and let's say it wasn't the same car when I'd finished! I squashed it, but the police were there and it was illegally parked. After I'd got my truck sorted, I noticed a car body shop on the estate, so

I walked in there and said, "Is that your car?" and they said, "No," to which I said, "It will be in a minute!"'

Suddenly Mark's effervescent demeanour darkens. 'I have seen a lot of accidents though, some minor, some not so minor. I saw a motorcyclist go under a lorry once, that wasn't very nice. But one crash springs to mind that really shook me up. I was following a van and I don't know what he did but he lost control, mounted the grass verge and then swerved and went straight into a lorry that had scaffolding poles on the trailer. One of the scaff poles went straight through him. I was the first person on the scene and he was absolutely mangled, so I dialled 999 and then tried to help him. I didn't know what to do so I put rags and bits of cloth on his head to stop the bleeding. I could hear the radio reports from my truck saying that he was dead. He wasn't but he was paralysed from the neck down.'

Fortunately Mark has yet to have a serious incident in his Stobart truck. 'I'd get my P45 if it was my fault. If I've put a lorry in a field and it's my fault, then I've lost my job, if it's driver negligence, or something stupid. But that applies to any business really.'

Despite the long hours, the solitary lifestyle, the demands of driving a massive truck and the stress of meeting Stobart's rigorously high standards, Mark loves his job: 'Twelve years I've been doing this and I am not bored with it yet, I'm nowhere near being past finished with this!' And will his tramping days always be with Stobart? 'I really do like working for them. Stobart is like a little family to me. It still feels like a family firm to me. I like having that name on the side of my trailer.' //

Behind the Wheel

A FIRST-HAND ACCOUNT OF A TRUCKING NOVICE TAKING TO THE WHEEL OF ONE OF EDDIE'S LEGENDARY VEHICLES.

Having spent the morning on a drop with Mark Dixon, I could already see how complex the job of an Eddie Stobart trucker was, in particular how demanding of one's driving skills even the most basic drop or collection could be. I'd already begun to sense the appeal of the open road but all this was just as a passenger; luckily for me, I was about to find out what it was like to actually drive an Eddie Stobart truck. I wanted the full experience so I started the day in the Stobart truckers' cafe at the Carlisle depot, enjoying a rather delicious Full English sat at a metal table, surrounded by drivers and well-thumbed copies of various tabloid newspapers.

//STAT

THE AVERAGE AGE OF THE STOBART GROUP VEHICLE IS JUST 18 MONTHS.

Before setting off, I'd also had a depot tour with Andrew Kidd, who is in charge of the fan club. Andrew's effervescent enthusiasm for the company was very clear, as he told me all manner of fascinating statistics and stories as we wandered around the depot. There was a real sense of passion for his job and a belief in the company which he imbued in me, so by the time I was set to head out in a truck, I was even more excited.

The day's plan was for Mark to drive me to Carlisle Airport, which Eddie Stobart bought in 2009. By definition, the runways there were privately owned so I would be able to get behind the steering wheel of a 44-tonne truck that was normally only the preserve of fully qualified lorry drivers. Prior to this, the largest vehicles I had ever driven were a Transit van and a Morris Marina estate.

I'd become relatively relaxed riding in the passenger seat of Phoebe Grace, with Mark Dixon driving as he does so naturally. Lulled into a very false sense of security, his expertise made me wonder if I might be quite good at driving this huge vehicle after all. Carlisle Airport is a relatively modest affair situated to the northeast of the city just off the A689, between the Lake District, the Scottish Border country and the North Pennines. The airport is known as the 'Gateway to the Lakes and the South of Scotland'.

As we pulled up to the airport I heard a huge roar and looked in the sky to see three massive Chinook helicopters performing what appeared to be some kind of military exercise. We later found out that it was the Dutch army on training manoeuvres. After Mark had parked up, he snapped a couple of pictures of the huge choppers (he did say he loves anything that has an engine, remember?), then we walked across to the terminal building to get clearance for my drive. The helicopters were just heading off to some far-flung European airfield as we did so, which was a relief as the idea of driving an Eddie Stobart truck whilst surrounded by swarms of military helicopters had been both surreal and rather worrying at the same time!

A very amiable airport man escorted us out to the runway, driving ahead of Phoebe Grace in his air traffic control car. The yellow lights flashing on the roof raised my sense of expectation – and heartbeat – a few notches. He would shadow the truck at every moment, to make sure that we were not driving where and when we shouldn't. Both Mark and I got out and the Stobart veteran made a few reassuring comments before holding up his bunch of keys between us. The air must have been rarefied around Carlisle Airport, because my breathing was definitely a little more rapid when Mark looked at me with obvious trepidation on his face and said, 'I am now going to hand over my truck to someone who's never driven a lorry before. What am I doing?!'

Above: *From the driver's seat, the ground looks a long way away.*

Suitably unnerved, I pulled myself up into the driver's side of the cabin and sank down into the air-cushioned seat behind the wheel. The dashboard was utilitarian; a simple button on the side of the steering column released the steering wheel which could then move backwards and forwards at an angle, to suit each trucker's driving position.

I'd heard horror stories of trucks with 28 gears but thankfully this Volvo had an I-shift system, which could be operated in automatic and semi-automatic modes (not manual). I think Mark was more relieved about this than I was. He patiently explained the various controls and dials and then having checked the seat was correct for my driving position, suggested I start her up.

The 460bhp engine roared into life and my heart started racing even faster. I could feel the engine vibrating through the steering wheel and one thing that struck me instantly was how incredibly high I was. As a passenger you realise you are high but that has no relevance other than that it gives you a nice view. As the driver, it made me feel isolated, exposed, a long way from the safety of the ground. Perched up so high, I'd already started to feel I had no control whatsoever over the truck, and we hadn't even moved off yet.

'Off you go then, nice and slow,' said Mark, his voice still filled with trepidation. I gently pushed the accelerator pedal down and the truck obediently nudged forward, far more receptive to my foot's pressure than I had expected. The runway was indeed clear of helicopters now so the 'road' ahead was empty, which is just as well because I felt like I had no right to be driving this £75,000 machine.

Mark was understandably nervous with me in charge of his precious truck but he quelled those nerves and was very patient and encouraging. At first I drove the truck slowly in a straight line and then took a very wide turn at the end of the runway to head back to our starting point. The turning circle was sharper than I had expected but when I looked in the rear-view mirrors I started to realise how incredibly long the trailer behind me was. Although I had made the turn neatly, I had no idea where the trailer behind was actually moving and had there been anything in its path I would have certainly demolished it.

After a number of straight shuttles up and down the runway, Mark suggested we use the white lines in the centre of the airstrip for a little steering practice. After a few attempts I managed to get the trailer to weave in and out of this *ad hoc* slalom course quite well. By now I was in trucking heaven, putting my foot down and driving at around 30mph, which to me felt like 300mph. Fortunately, the brakes were very responsive too, biting their impact as soon as you pushed down the pedal.

'Right, you've got the hang of that, now it's time to reverse,' said Mark.

For my first reverse, my 'loading bay' was in fact an expanse of wide runway with no buildings or vehicles for hundreds of metres. I'd heard that some reverses are tougher than others. The most difficult manoeuvre in a truck is the so-called 'blindside reverse' where the driver can't actually see what is in the blindspot over the left shoulder, even with the seven mirrors each truck has. Worse still is 'blindsiding' into a tight bay, where the margin for error is tiny, usually a matter of inches. Thankfully, I had no such obstacles, but I was still anxious to do well.

STAT//

A 'SPOT' IS ONLY COUNTED WHEN THE VEHICLE IS COMMISSIONED INTO SERVICE AND IN FULL ESL OR CUSTOMER LIVERY.

Mark kindly negotiated the truck into a position at a right angle to a section of runway which he wanted me to reverse into. Suitably buoyed by my 'breakneck' speeds in a straight line, I started to reverse, looking out of my mirrors and feeling for all the world like an Eddie Stobart driver on a drop. But that's when it all started to go horribly wrong. It's hard to understand how the tiniest of movements on the steering wheel up front can lead to an enormous shift in the position of the trailer, more than 13 metres behind me. On the one hand, everything you have to do is exaggerated, over-sized, but by contrast the smallest of errors on the wheel can have disastrous consequences at the rear. As Mark was about to find out.

Within about ten seconds of starting my first reversing manoeuvre, the trailer had kicked into a complete right angle – the dreaded jack-knife position – and the tyres were screeching in protest as my cab tried to force the trailer into an angle that it could not cope with. I also noticed that on the passenger's side I was completely blind, there could have been an entire Tesco store there and I wouldn't have known.

How do they do this?

'Let's try again,' said Mark, patiently.

We set the truck up again and Mark gently explained where I was going wrong. The obvious point to make is that the trailer goes in the opposite direction to that in which you turn the wheel. Once you get your head around that counter-intuitive notion, the next difficulty is to not over-steer; the tendency to make adjustments that are magnified along the length of the trailer and lead to a problem is difficult to overcome. Also, at times the trailer is in the correct position and you actually don't need to steer at all, it almost manoeuvres itself. But knowing when this is the case and how much to steer etc, is all part of the secret.

On a couple of attempts, Mark took the wheel while I pushed the pedal down, and as he did so he explained what he was doing. Then it would be my turn but no matter how much I concentrated and tried to remember what he'd just told me,

//STAT

Stobart's biggest warehouses can store as many as 100,000 pallets at any one time.

it never seemed to be quite as easy! We repeated the reverse over and over until eventually I got the trailer roughly in the direction of where he'd wanted to go.

By now my mind was actually swimming with the tips and hints he'd given me, so I asked if he would reverse it in to show me how it was done. We'd earlier set a white line on the runway as the rear limit of the trailer's fictitious 'loading bay' and within about ten seconds of climbing behind the wheel, Mark had parked the trailer inch-perfect next to the line, as if he'd picked it up by hand and carefully placed it there himself. Surely resisting the temptation to say, 'That's how it's done', Mark commended me on my efforts and said I was 'Not bad at all.' Somehow I don't think Eddie Stobart will be offering me a job any time soon.

After we had finished, Mark – visibly relieved to have the keys to Phoebe Grace back in his hand – guided the truck to the safe parking area outside the runway so that we could grab a cup of tea and a bite to eat in the cafe. As he parked his truck, I was now acutely aware of the skill involved in this apparently simple manoeuvre, while Mark just chatted away, instinctively moving the truck precisely where he needed it to go. I asked him how he knew where to stop as the angle of parking had meant we couldn't easily see the end of the trailer by the control tower. 'Shadows,' he said, 'you can sometimes work out where you need to go with the trailer's shadow.'

We walked into the cafe and while waiting for a cup of tea chatted with some plane-spotters who were enjoying the sunshine outside and were thrilled by the Dutch helicopters they'd seen an hour earlier. I was a little embarrassed when it became apparent they had also been watching my stuttering attempts to reverse Mark's truck. Eventually, one of them, a qualified pilot as it transpired, politely and with a look of genuine amusement, turned to me and said, 'You're not a truck driver then!' //

STANDARD STOBART VOLVO FH460

The popular Volvo FH460 has a 13-litre, 460bhp engine that is restricted to 56mph by law. The truck and trailer combined stretch 16.5 metres maximum. Cruise control and traction control for slippery ground increase efficiency and safety, while inside the complex GPS system Isotrack sends exact details of each truck's progress to the relevant planner's office.

   The front of the radiator grille can fold down to make an impromptu seat, while many drivers often store their deckchairs behind the cab. When these cabs (sometimes called 'tractor units') are driving without a trailer hitched, they are said to be 'solo'.

No Dead Mileage

How Stobart transformed their business post-2004 from an iconic haulage firm into a modern-day giant of multi-modal logistics expertise.

So the post-2004 revival of Eddie Stobart has been fuelled by the arrival of several key new ventures, including rail, airports, ports and international divisions. Another highly topical and contemporary new area is Stobart Biomass division, established in 2010. Biomass is essentially the transport and movement of recycled materials, most obviously wood, garden waste, peats, etc. The strict definition of biomass is 'a renewable energy source derived from living material or recently living material such as wood or plant waste'. This means items such as dead trees, branches, tree stumps, garden clippings, woodchip, waste (and sometimes sustainable) wood, also defined as 'expired timber product, forestry residue and compostable matter, as well as plant or animal matter.' The last can include such unpleasant items as chicken faeces! With the government aiming to have 30 per cent of all electricity generated this way by 2020, biomass is a growing market.

The biomass material is usually either burnt in huge incinerators to make fuel for green power stations, or alternatively (in the case of the wood) shredded and made into furniture chipboard for Britain's kitchens and bedrooms. Previously, this material would have simply been discarded into landfill. Typically these power stations might require 1,250 tonnes of biomass each and every day, which is the equivalent of about sixty to eighty trucks filled to bursting.

This new division required a fleet of specially manufactured trucks designed to tap into this growing market for recyclable materials. At the time of writing, Stobart deliver 23,000 tonnes of waste wood every week. Having been with Mark Dixon on a more conventional curtain-sided lorry previously, I was now due to do a drop with a Biomass truck. Back at the Carlisle depot, Mark walked me over to a truck called Sarah Gabriella inside which I could see a familiar face, another of Stobart's well-known drivers, Tim Fox. He was busily tidying up his cabin ahead of my arrival and, after asking me to excuse the mess (I couldn't see any), he opened the door for me and I climbed up, wishing Mark farewell as I did so. I clambered into the cabin and shook hands with the driver known as 'The Biomass Maestro'.

As we pulled away from the depot, I started off by asking if it was true that Stobart Biomass drivers were indeed more experienced than most. 'I'm always reluctant to say I'm more experienced,' replied Tim in his colourful Bury accent, 'because I can drive a particular stretch of motorway every day for the rest of me life and yet every time I do, it's like a different stretch because it's not the same cars, it's not the same conditions. People think they are experienced, but there's nothing to say I won't have an accident on a stretch of road I've driven for years.'

Tim's being modest though; he has been trucking for 27 years when I interview him and like so many of the Stobart drivers I meet, he's the latest in a long family tradition. Tim's knowledge of his own father's driving past sheds a fascinating light on how the industry has changed and Stobart own pivotal role in that transformation and modernisation: 'I wanted to drive a truck from the day I could

Left: *Stobart veteran Tim Fox, who specialises in their Biomass division work.*
Below: *Biomass represents a booming market for Stobart, with their fleet moving 23,000 tonnes of waste every week.*

talk. Me dad was a truck driver and it's all I ever wanted to do, I've never wanted to do anything else. Dad had done his years tramping up and down the motorways, so – like me now – he was out a lot. When you go back to the 1970s, there were loads of independent truck companies with just a few trucks each. So back then, you could have a fall-out with one manager, walk out of that job and straight into another.

'I can remember me dad's wagon being made of wood. Tongue-and-groove. old AACs, Albions, Scammells, they'd pretty much just got hold of a chassis and an engine and made the cab themselves. The power steering was your bicep! Nowadays the trucks have got everything you could want, a microwave, fridge, bed, TV, 240-volt for your iPad, laptop, power steering, the works. Dad lived through the really old days of trucking and into the modern era and as a boy alongside him I was lucky enough to see some of that too. He always admired Stobart. He liked the fact they were so smart and that they did things properly.

'I used to go out with me dad all the time. I could tie a dolly [a knot for use when securing truck loads and tying off sheets] at six. There's not many drivers now that can rope and sheet a 45-foot trailer fast, it's a dying art, but I was learning that with me dad way back when I was a kid. I was about eleven when he started tramping. There were a lot of steelworks in South Wales and he'd do a lot of drops around there, so I'd often jump in with him and then we'd go and see me aunty in St Ives!'

Such fond childhood memories clearly fuel Tim's passion for his job: 'It's a good life, it's all I've ever done. When I first left school I did a couple of years as an apprentice diesel mechanic, looking after all the wagons, but that was just me biding time till I could get my licence. As soon as I turned 17 I got me licence and started driving a seven-and-a-half tonner, and that was it, I was off. I couldn't get my Class 1 fast enough. I passed my heavy goods in 1993. I was itching to get out there. I'd only been passed a week and they asked me to pick up a hay trailer from Bury. They were expecting me to cock it up, but because I'd done two years fixing trucks, I'd spent hours and hours reversing them into the garage, into really tight spots. So on the first day I went down there, picked the trailer up, went back and reversed it straight in! All the lads in the yard were watching, waiting for me to cock it up but she went straight in. The boss were like, "I can't believe you did that!"'

Tim remembers his early days as if they were yesterday. 'My first solo drop was taking a load to Holland & Barrett. I was driving an old Ford D series, that lorry were horrible! The brakes… well, they weren't really brakes, they were more like an on-and-off switch! For my first night out in a truck, I parked up at an old cafe on the A47 going to Norwich. I had to sleep across the seats, because there were no bed. It only had an old quilt, but it were alright actually! It was so exciting! That was all I wanted to do and I'd finally done it.'

By now Tim's truck had left the A-roads around Carlisle and we were heading up the last few yards of the M6, eventually driving northwest along the A76 to our destination not far from the coast, west of Glasgow. I'd already noticed the obstacles and problems with narrow roads, parked cars and tiny entrances when I had been out with Mark on A-roads and housing estates, but now on the motorways I became very aware of the unpredictable nature of traffic. As we passed under various motorway signs, one flashed a warning of delays ahead and I could easily see how the slightest unforeseen problem could have a very negative knock-on effect in a busy day of multiple deliveries. Fortunately, Tim's full load of wood refuse was starting out on a long journey for a single drop, so by comparison it seemed a simple drive.

That is, it would have been simple if we had stayed on the motorway. However, after a few miles, we turned off and headed up a series of A-roads, several of which ran through small villages, packed with old-fashioned shops on either side, parked cars, zebra crossings and viciously unforgiving sharp turns.

STAT//

THE 'SPOTTER LEAGUE TABLE' IS COMPILED USING UNIQUE 'SPOTS', UPDATED AND POSTED ON THE WEBSITE. THERE IS ALSO A SPOTTER'S JOURNAL WHERE AVID FOLLOWERS CAN UPLOAD RECENT SIGHTINGS.

Opposite: *Biomass drivers have to be prepared for unusual and treacherous terrain.*

The scenery was spectacular, and once again I began to see why trampers enjoy life on the road. Tim seemed to read my mind as he explained why he loves his job: 'The freedom. There's nobody looking over my shoulder. Alright, you've got a phone and they need to know where you are, of course, in fact with all the GPS systems they can tell exactly where I am, what speed I'm doing, they can even tell how many revs I'm running! But even with all that they give you the work and I go off and do it.'

After around 90 minutes we arrived at a remote logging factory, and after waiting for one truck ahead of us to complete his drop, we headed into a vast yard filled with mountains of either fine woodchip or recycled scraps of wood, mountains made from bits of old furniture, household scraps, the remnants of a kid's cricket bat, all sorts. The mountains were 20 to 30 feet high, towering above the truck which for once seemed tiny by comparison.

Tim's truck is not just any Stobart lorry. Much of the main fleet are so-called 'chipliners'. This means they have a curtain side that is specifically made to carry loose loads. You can recognise one of these chipliners on the roads because the sides of the curtain will be bulging out, rather than perfectly taut as with more normal loads. Chipliner drivers have to pay particular attention to how tight the curtain clips on either side are!

Biomass trucks have wheels across six axles, power steering and an engine of usually 440bhp. Despite the power, these lorries have a very good Euro 5-rated lower emissions level, entirely in keeping with the ecological nature of their work.

Like all Stobart Biomass trucks, Tim's is solid-sided (not a curtain-sider), and is equipped with a so-called 'walking floor'. This innovation replaced the older system whereby the trailer was hoisted into the air by a hydraulic arm built into it. Stobart have always been quick to adopt new technology: in 1996 they were the first haulage firm in the UK to own these previously-used tipping trailers which had been designed in-house and built with the help of Montracon.

//STAT

IN 2012, CORGI LAUNCHED
TWO DETAILED DIE-CAST
MODELS TO MARK THE FIRST
ANNIVERSARY OF EDWARD'S
DEATH. THE SET FEATURES DIE-
CAST MODELS OF THE SCANIA
4 SERIES WITH A CURTAIN-
SIDE TRAILER, THE SCANIA
111 'JULIA' AND *THE EDWARD
STOBART STORY*, A BOOKLET
ABOUT THE FIRM.

The walking floor consists of a number of longitudinal slats which move backwards and forwards in an alternating sequence, thus pushing the load along the bed of the trailer and out of the end. The trailers also have roll-top roofs and usually curtain sides, so that the material can be dumped in easily and extracted quickly if a dumper truck chooses to push the load out sideways instead. Special care has to be taken not to drop heavy or sharp objects onto the trailer's soft aluminium floor.

We parked up and Tim donned a special dust-proof mask and told me I wasn't allowed outside for health and safety reasons – I was quietly pleased! – and he then stepped out into a cloud of dust and noise. Around us water hoses sprayed a fine haze of water to try to keep the storms of dust down. As he opened up his trailer, the cabin shunted from side to side as the noises and bangs prepared us for offloading.

To access the roll-top roof, Tim had to climb up a very narrow ladder which is pinned between the front of the trailer and the cabin. As I watched Tim ascend in my rear view mirror, he made it clear there wasn't much room for maneouvre by sucking in his cheeks and patting his stomach, all done with a smile of course. He attached himself to a safety harness that was fixed to a metal gantry, some 15 feet in the air, which keeps drivers safe should they slip off while peeling back the roof.

As he was getting the truck ready, there was an almighty roar and a dumper truck the size of which I have never seen before screeched out of the factory. Now I realised why I wasn't allowed outside the cabin: this thing was monstrous and I later found out that each scoop of its enormous bucket could pick up 1.5 tonnes of woodchip. It is massive. If we were picking up a load of woodchip, the trailer would be full in just 20 scoops.

The truck's walking floor began its ingenious work and shuffled the 27-tonne load of woodchip along and out of the rear end of the trailer in around seven minutes; Tim teased the process along by occasionally edging his lorry forward very slowly. 'It's like a 45-foot Weetabix,' he told me. It is indeed, but when burnt in the incinerator, that wood chip will be able to provide electricity to 30,000 homes for an hour. Not even Weetabix can do that.

When the offloading was completed, Tim swept the dust off his precious empty trailer and closed up the back. The air was still thick with dust and the floor was covered in a dense blanket of splinters. The smell of cut wood was almost overpowering. Tim assured me that this is the nicest smell he has to put up with and suggested I was lucky we were not on a drop at a compost farm.

Above: *Biomass trucks are fitted with a 'walking floor' which pushes the load out of the back of the trailer.*

'You get a lot of punctures on the biomass wagons because you are going to wood depots, there's nails, shards of wood and all that, everywhere. But I have noticed punctures come in threes! Always in threes, why is that? Once I had two punctures on me wagon in a week and it was really difficult to get my work done, then I dropped off the truck on the Friday and walked to me car to go home and I had a puncture on that!'

Does the biomass work mean Tim's had some weird loads? 'You get a fair few rats and snakes in the biomass. It's a huge pile of woodchip, it's warm so they tuck up in there and go to sleep. They can get a little bit annoyed when they get woke up early! I've seen much worse though! Once I was parked behind a driver and I looked ahead and thought, There's some trainers hanging off his back axle! I thought they were messing about, sometimes lads will disconnect your trailer while you are asleep, nice and quiet, and drop it down safely then you drive off in the morning without doing your checks and you will go without your trailer attached. So I just thought someone was messing about. But then I looked again and these trainers moved! 'Ey up! So I shouted to the driver and it turned out there was a bloke under the wagon. He'd run up behind the lorry with a piece of hardboard and he was lying on the axles with this plank.' At least they were in the right place to recycle the sheet of wood.

Joking aside, if an illegal immigrant is found inside a British truck the vehicle's owner can be fined £2,000 per person discovered. This is a particular problem

Top: *Woodchip is one of the staple loads of the Biomass fleet and is used for both furniture manufacture and incineration.*
Left: *Unsurprisingly, Biomass trucks suffer a high number of punctures from the problematic sites they visit.*

for the drivers who cross the Channel – with one million trucks passing through Calais alone each year, the opportunities for illegal immigrants to stow away on board are high. Heat-sensing equipment at each port helps find stowaways and there are strict regulations in place, but the driver always has to be on guard.

Back at the wood factory, Tim restarted his engine, moved us out of the way and parked up to watch the dumper. In about three scoops, every single piece of woodchip that this huge truck had deposited was swiftly pushed into the nearest mountain. With a parp of his horn, we were done and on our way.

As we pulled away, I noticed some scaffolding climbing up the side of one of the factory's walls and I recalled Mark Dixon witnessing a metal pole impaling a van driver. So I asked if Tim had ever seen a bad smash. He had – it seems the road veterans have all had their share of shocking incidents while clocking up so many miles. For the only time that day, Tim's indefatigable good humour diminished. 'I was driving in Germany one time and I tried to get a bloke out of a burning truck but I couldn't get him out. Three of us were trying to but we couldn't get to him.

'Afterwards I rang the gaffer up and he cancelled my next day's work, so I parked up and got blind drunk that night. That knocked me back for a bit, but you can't let it worry you, so you have to get on with your job. I'm not a religious man, but I believe in fate and so I try not to worry about those things.'

Keen to lighten the mood, which isn't hard with Tim as he is one of the most jovial people I've ever met, I ask him why he came to work for Stobart. Was it the clean trucks and immaculate uniform? The excellent reputation or maybe the state-of-the-art trucks? 'To be totally brutally honest, I was in Bristol parked up next to one of their drivers and he showed me his pay slip! That made me mind up! I love my job, but you don't know what a firm is actually like until you work for them. For me personally they are fantastic, they let me get on with it, there's no screaming and shouting. We just get on and do it. And I could start an argument in a mirror so that's saying something!'

STAT//

IF THE PRICE OF DIESEL GOES UP BY £0.01, THAT REPRESENTS AN EXTRA COST TO STOBART OF APPROXIMATELY £1 MILLION.

On the long journey back to Carlisle, I notice as a passenger in this huge truck how many times we are overtaken, often in dangerous places and occasionally with the odd two-fingered gesture from an annoyed car driver. With all UK HGVs limited to just 56mph, they are often the subject of frustrated drivers trying but failing to pass them on windy A-roads. Ironically, truck drivers on a tight schedule loathe being behind the dreaded tractor, which is known in the trade as 'a dirty wheeler'. I wonder what a tractor driver hates being caught behind?

Tim seems completely unfazed by these unpredictable overtakers but one aspect that does frustrate him is the lack of awareness among the public about what driving a 44-tonne truck entails. 'The biggest eye-opener for a member of the public sat in here is the amount of space you need on the road to make turns, especially tight turns. Particularly a left-hand turn, you haven't got the space to get the trailer round. People don't realise that you need to take it so wide. The sheer bulk of the thing is massive. It's very rare that the public allow you the space; people will often try and nip round you when you've stopped to turn. Sometimes they even try to nip round you when you've started reversing! That can be frustrating. They are not doing it on purpose, they just don't know how much space we need. It makes it hard not to get your hair off, but they've never driven a truck in their lives. But it feels like there's less patience out there and people do take a chance to get past you.'

Even though Tim still thinks he has the dream job, he's not in denial about other negatives: 'It's hard to balance family life sometimes, admittedly. I stayed at home for about three years but eventually I went back to tramping, it's what I am. But if my wife turned around to me tomorrow and asked me to stop, I would, I'd be on days as soon as they could arrange it. She lets me do this job, she's always let me do the job and I won't give me marriage up for any job, but a lot of drivers do, it kills marriages, this job. It's a marriage wrecker; they get cab happy, it's all they can do, they just want to be in the wagon all the time. I've seen drivers where they

*A drop at a logging factory
or refuse site is frequently
protracted, often dangerous
and always dirty.*

TRUCK DUMPER

With Biomass, the walking floor is a very efficient way to tip a load; another regular method is to push the woodchip or other materials through the side of the open trailer with a dumper. There is, however, another far more spectacular approach: the so-called truck dumper.

This £500,000 piece of kit literally tips the lorry up on its back end, raising the nose up to seventy degrees, at which point the cabin is perched high in the air. Of course, this way gravity helps and the entire load can be discharged very swiftly.

An obvious question would be how dangerous is it to lift a 44-tonne truck so high in the air? Fortunately, the hydraulic lifting device on the truck dumper is so safe that even if the pipes were cut, it would not crash to the floor, but would instead simply halt where it was. Also, its 160KW of power means it actually has the capacity to lift 60 tonnes, so the Stobart trucks are lightweights!

can't wait to get back in. I know that feeling. If I'm off for two weeks I'm aching to get back to my world, in the wagon, get back in here, get to work. This is normality for me.'

It's clearly not like this for everyone though, as Tim explains: 'I've seen blokes in tears because they can't hack tramping. One time in Gibraltar I came across a lad in a wagon and he was in tears. He got there, he'd got lost going down, he'd had to pay for his own tolls because his boss had said he couldn't use them [Stobart pay £1 million a year in tolls], he had all this trouble finding his way down and so by the time he got there his heart had gone. He just left the wagon there and flew home. You also see day lads who try tramping but can't manage it. You can generally tell a tramper a mile off – maybe it's because they smell of sweat! No, seriously, I think it's just in you, it's hard to say what it is, you can look at a driver and know he's a tramper. It's a certain breed.'

The longer a drop is away from base the more a tramper likes the job: 'You get given what you are given, obviously. A crap job is all half-hour journeys, you load it all up, but you are tipping only half an hour down the road, it's just too bitty. I like the long runs, a day's run ideally, I prefer that type of work, I'd quite happily pick up at John O'Groats and deliver to Land's End every day. It's surprising how far you can get in nine hours a day.'

I ask Tim about Stobart's standing among its peers and rivals, in particular with regard to the introduction of the uniform. Again, his long-standing involvement in the industry provides a telling insight: 'There were firms out there who were smart, but not like Stobart with a tie and a shirt. You might have had an overall in a certain colour or something like that but not specific uniforms like Edward introduced. I wasn't bothered though when I was a kid, at 18 you could have made me dress in bin bags, as long as I had the keys to a wagon, I weren't bothered. It was jeans and T-shirt. But now, you can see why it worked. The job's gone from a labouring job to a profession, you are a professional driver. The police will actually

STAT//

THE STOBART FIRETRUCK USED AT THEIR AIRPORTS CAN CARRY THE EQUIVALENT OF 125 BATHFULS OF WATER.

say that to you, "You should know better, you are a professional". And I do, I see myself as a professional driver. I understand why they wanted to get that image, it's important. Stobart played a big role in that.

'Edward Stobart transformed the way hauliers worked. It wasn't unique to have beautiful trucks. There were some beautiful signwritten liveries out there back in the day other than Stobart, to be fair, some really amazing stuff, so I thought a lot of trucks looked fantastic. For me, it was more about the way he presented the drivers, that was unique. The attitude he drummed into them, you don't turn up with a fag in your mouth and your arse hanging out your pants. You go in with your manners, you have to be very presentable… that word again, professional.

'Before I drove for Stobart, I used to do international runs for another firm. We use to take the mickey out of Stobart drivers summat terrible at the ports. We used to rip 'em to pieces. We were all there in flip-flops and shorts, T-shirts, and they'd turn up in uniforms and ties. Some of us even had company-coloured boiler suits or shirts, but if you were going to Spain and it was baking hot, you just didn't wear them. Stobart drivers always did.' Tim admits that today there is still sometimes 'anti-Eddie' sentiment out there among other drivers and rival firms; while fellow Eddie truckers wave at each other, rival firms will often give a rather more direct two-fingered salute.

'Back then they stood out like sore thumbs. But now, you look back and I would say 90 per cent of those firms we were driving for, them firms aren't there anymore. The reason Stobart is still here is because Edward raised the standards.

'It's like you were telling me earlier about what you'd learned driving Mark's wagon. A small turn on the wheel makes a vast difference at the back. That's what Edward did. He made a lot of small changes but they made a huge difference. Very clever. Put the driver in clean clothes, that's not hard, but just that one thing alone had a massive impact. Take that dirty oily vest and boots off him, make him have a wash now and then. Trust me, there's some dirty bloody drivers out there, you sit

LOGGING LORRY

Another sustainable industry that Stobart has entered post-2004 is logging. In Scotland this trade is worth nearly £2 billion, but as yet the fleet only has one logging lorry, Laura Jane (H8237). This V8, 500bhp truck is extra-powerful so as to be able to negotiate the muddy and slippy forest tracks that it has to use. The tyres are strengthened to be more puncture-resistant due to the high number of splinters and shards of wood, and the thick treads offer a better grip in the mud.

Laura Jane comprises an SDC chassis with a log lift and bolsters, all pulled by a Scania R500 V8 cab. She has an elevating cab attached to the front of the trailer that works a huge claw, itself capable of rotating 360 degrees to pick up a tonne of logs at a time. The logs are hoisted and placed on the trailer, where they are kept in place by high-strength aluminium posts. Each section is movable, so that the first load can slide up to the front of the trailer to make way for the next load. Fully loaded, the lorry can carry 25 tonnes of timber.

STOBART'S GREENER TRUCKS

Another way that Stobart are pushing the boundaries of 'green trucking' is with liquified natural gas (LNG)trucks. There are 25 of these £100,000 trucks in the fleet and their 13-litre, 460bhp engines are capable of running both diesel and LPG. They are known as 'Dual fuel eco trucks'. The fuel is liquefied gas, stored in special tanks at minus 162 degrees centigrade; they have a range of 500 miles. With only four LNG truck refuelling stations in the UK, the lorries inevitably run out on occasion, and this is when the computers inside will seamlessly switch the engine to running on standard diesel. This might seem an expensive and tricky way to run a truck but these lorries use a third less diesel than a standard truck and thus substantially reduce carbon emissions.

Another push for lower-emission trucking came in 2012 when Stobart took their first ever delivery of a new longer trailer: the so-called Envirotrailer. Under new regulations aimed at being more green, temporary trial laws allowed higher volume trailers. The hope is to cut emissions, slash carbon footprints and boost fleet economy. This 15.65 metre trailer (the standard trailer length is 13.6 metres) has two steering rear axles, allowing a 20 per cent increase in payload. Stobart Envirotrailer is operated under a special licence as part of a ten-year trial.

There are other 'green' options too. The fleet is constantly trying to reduce so-called 'empty miles', namely those where a truck is travelling with an empty trailer, wasting money and also harming the environment. Between 2006 and 2011 Stobart planning offices managed to cut these wasteful empty miles by 50 per cent. The average Stobart truck is fully loaded for 85 per cent of its lifetime mileage; for every 1 per cent of this so-called 'increased fleet utilisation', carbon emissions are reduced by 1107 tonnes.

in cafes and sometimes they have flies buzzing round them! Even though the word 'tramper' has nothing to do with the word tramp! So small changes, but a massive impact.'

So is Tim a tramper for life? 'I'd love to go into the training side when I'm older. I feel I have got something to offer, to put back in from nearly 30 years of haulage experience. I've driven all over Europe, so I feel like when my time comes and I've had enough of sleeping in a wagon all week, that's what I'd like to do. Teach the young 'uns how to drive. But I'd like to do it for Stobart because I like the way they operate.'

STOBART DRIVER BONUS SCHEME

As part of Stobart's drive for efficiency – in both its own fiscal interests and also from an emissions point of view – the company has a bonus scheme that rewards careful driving. With the omnipresent Isotrack system monitoring exactly where, when, how fast and how long a driver is moving, there is a bonus on offer for those who do not log so-called 'faults'. These faults might include revving too hard, braking too sharply, accelerating too fast, too much idling of the engine and so on. There is a green band on the dashboard and the idea is to keep the needle in this and out of the red!

Each day a driver is given one hundred bonus points with deductions being made for each fault. At the end of a week, if the driver has preserved a certain number of points then they are awarded their bonus, which can be as high as £3.50 a day – this sounds modest but over a year that can add up to a five-figure sum. Usually around 65 per cent of drivers secure a bonus. //

The Chilled Division

How the Stobart empire has pushed the boundaries of trucking in more ways than just uniforms and spotless trucks — reinventing logistics and rewriting the rulebooks.

Edward Stobart realised back in the 1970s that for his firm to expand he needed to look beyond the 'dirty' loads of coal and slag; equally, after the 2004 takeover by William and Andrew, the duo were eager to diversify their fleet's capabilities. The Biomass truck of Tim Fox is a classic example of this widening of the Stobart remit. As well as being a torch-bearer for Stobart's proactive adoption of new technology, the ever-expanding Biomass fleet also symbolises the firm's attitude to success: never content with just being the best in the business, they are constantly striving to open up new frontiers in other, related areas.

Above: *Stobart chilled trailers are essentially colossal moving fridges, restocking the shelves of the nation's supermarkets.*

Another of the company's most active new sectors is the chilled food division, nattily titled 'Temperature Controlled Distribution'. Launched in the spring of 1999 with just twenty trailers, Stobart now has ten chilled food depots across the UK and 350–400 chilled food drivers available at any one time, who in total deliver 70,000 pallets of fresh food every week. This adds up to 3.5 million pallets each year, which represents over one million tonnes of perishable goods. Britain's supermarkets would almost grind to a halt if Stobart's chilled division stopped work. Their chilled depot headquarters in Appleton controls a business worth almost £100 million a year to the firm. Each chilled depot has specially designed warehouse space with massive refrigeration units inside, capable of keeping the temperature at a perfect level to preserve the fresh goods.

The thermally-insulated refrigerated trailer units are designed to maintain a perfect temperature for fresh food while it is being delivered. The most modern are called Insuliners and were introduced in 2010. Usually a chilled delivery is timed within half an hour so that the integrity of the goods is not jeopardised. Many of the chilled drivers are night-shift workers (Stobart has around 750 night drivers in total), delivering food for the nation while it sleeps, with a regular flurry of work before each weekend. Also, due to the very nature of the delivery customer – many city-centre supermarkets and often quite small independent shops – the chilled-division driver has to be used to multi-drops, where each day brings multiple destinations and split loads and collections. Multi-drops are high tempo and high volume, all very local but very fast: 'One bad drop and your day is pretty much screwed,' as one driver told me.

URBAN CHILL TRAILER

The so-called 'chill trailer' is ten metres long, which makes it shorter and more manoeuvrable than its heftier curtain-sided counterparts. Each trailer can be divided internally into three separate compartments so that different foodstuffs can be stored at different temperatures, ranging from minus 20 to plus 20 degrees centigrade for split loads, as required.

Each trailer has a mechanised tail lift powered by the detachable trailer which is vital for dropping off cages full of heavy food at supermarkets that are often based in very busy city centres. The trailers alone cost £57,000 each.

Recent technological advances have meant that a curtain-sider has been designed that is capable of carrying chilled foodstuffs. This is possible thanks to a special two-inch thick curtain that is admittedly very heavy to pull back but has the benefit of acting like a rigid wall. In this way, Stobart are able to load/ tip the foodstuffs from the side using forklifts, instead of the slower method of pushing the usual cages in or out via the rear opening. This can drastically reduce loading and tipping times, thus saving money: two forklifts can fully load a chilled curtain-sider in just five minutes. These special trailers have the huge bonus that they can be used for standard, non-chilled loads too, which means they are working 24/7 – as against the standard rear-opening chilled trailer which frequently has very busy periods of use before and during a weekend, but can often lie idle in the first part of the week.

By contrast, Eddie Stobart has a fleet of heated trailers, which can control the temperature inside to keep perishable goods above a certain point; these vehicles are typically used for plants and garden stock.

The chilled division has to move vast quantities of perishable goods very quickly, or risk heavy losses and customer dissatisfaction.

FIONA: 'THE NATION'S FAVOURITE FEMALE TRUCKER'

One of the chilled division's highest-profile drivers is Fiona Soltysiak. Her path to driving an Eddie Stobart truck is a fascinating one and sheds light on the industry as a whole, in particular how Stobart's eagerness to encourage female drivers is not entirely endemic.

Above: *Blazing a trail: Fiona Soltysiak.*

Like so many of her fellow drivers, Fiona's father was in the Forces so her childhood was an itinerant one. She felt at home only when constantly moving around. But it was not trucks that she dreamt of as a young girl: 'From school I knew I would work with horses; that was all I wanted to do. I studied them at college and I never ever thought about driving a lorry. To be honest, lorries petrified me when I was in a car, being next to these massive trucks, could they even see me?'

As soon as she was old enough, Fiona got work in a stable and pretty soon she was driving Land Rover Discoverys with trailers all day, manoeuvring them in and out of very small yards easily. 'I'd driven small trucks around the yard too, so these bigger vehicles weren't alien to me, but I got no enjoyment from them, they didn't thrill me. I wondered why this was and one day I realised it was because they weren't big enough!'

Her curiosity for a bigger vehicle was enhanced when she read an article in *Horse & Hound* magazine that pointed out how few female horse grooms could drive the large vehicles that are so essential to any stable, and she thought there might be a career in it for her. She soon qualified to drive a rigid truck with an HGV2 licence but even that wasn't big enough. 'I hated driving the 13-tonne rigid. I still got nothing from it and I was hitting every kerb you can imagine!'

One afternoon she was allowed to drive an artic around a private industrial estate by her boss and although she had been craving a big vehicle for some time, she was still shocked by just how big the truck was. 'But I drove it patiently and it was ace! Fifteen months later I found a City & Guilds offer to pay half of the costs of the HGV1 test and so I took lessons for a week and passed. I had my Class 1.'

Above: *The self-confessed 'girly girl' is not your typical trucker!*

Her determination had paid off and she was now qualified to drive articulated lorries at the young age of 25. However she still hadn't thought of trucking as a career, having only taken her Class 1 so that she would be able to get more work with horses.

'Three months later I heard of a firm in Newark taking on drivers and so I drove down there in my pink Golf Cabriolet, leather riding boots and jodhpurs, and my hair in pigtails, straight from a smelly horse yard. I walked up to someone and said, "Can you tell me where the drivers' manager is please?" and they said, "The office is that way, love . . ." I said, "I don't want the office, I've come here to drive!"

'I preferred to drive a truck with gears, which they only had available with a double-decker trailer. I took it out to test-drive for the firm and two weeks later they phoned and told me I'd got the job. That firm was then taken over by Stobart and so now I was driving for Eddie!' For the first couple of drops, like everyone else, Fiona was chaperoned. 'I had never driven past Leeds before! I didn't even take my car driving test until 2004, I'd grown up in a small village so I didn't need anything more than a moped. Now I was driving HGVs for a living!'

Before Stobart took over, Fiona did find that the preconceptions about female drivers in general, and especially female truck drivers, were all too real. 'Nobody spoke to me for three months, the whole depot was weird with me, the entire period until Stobart took over. Eventually when they did start speaking to me, they said they didn't think I'd last for more than a month, they'd even took bets on how long I'd handle it for. Eventually people started to realise I was sticking around and began speaking to me. It took a good year before everyone settled into the fact I was staying.

'I'm something of a girly girl, I drive a pink car, I've got ponies at home. That image fitted all their preconceptions and they just didn't expect me to last. But I knew I would: I'd been lugging around tonnes of horse poo and driving horseboxes for ages, so it wasn't physically any harder working their wagons than what I'd been doing before. Sometimes they'd see me pulling a cage and say, "Can you manage that?" and I'd think, I don't see you asking that 60-year-old driver if he needs any help!

'When I go to some depots, I often walk in and they stop me and literally say, "But you are not the driver!" I get that even when I've got the keys in my hand and sometimes even when they've seen me drive the truck in to the depot! They just can't fathom it out. At some places, all the factory workers will come out and if there's a particularly tricky bay, they will deliberately give it to me and then stand there watching to see if I can do it. I reverse in and can see all these people watching, then if I do it right when I get out of the cab they've all walked off!'

Even though Eddie Stobart actively encourage female drivers to apply, there are still only 14 women truckers out of a fleet total of over 4,000 at the time of writing. In the haulage industry as a whole, less than 1 per cent of drivers are women. This minority status creates one particular difficulty for Fiona which she light-heartedly explains: 'I moan about the uniform every day! The shirts came in collar sizes only, but females don't shop in collar sizes! Female office staff get a fitted blouse shirt and proper cut trousers, but as a lorry driver you just get the men's uniform. I've been hassling them to change that!

'I get up at 2.20 a.m. every day to get to work for 4 a.m. It's a long day but really enjoyable. I get home in the afternoons so I can ride my horse, pick my daughter up, live more of a normal life. Now I've got a full bike licence too, I own a big Suzuki motorbike which I've had wrapped in magenta bright pink. I'm trying to get Stobart to wrap a truck in pink too, but no luck so far!' //

STAT//

THE DAVENTRY DEPOT COVERS 60 ACRES, OR THE EQUIVALENT OF 20 WEMBLEY STADIUMS.

Keeping the Fleet Moving

Stobart is famous for logistical expertise, yet the sheer number of its vehicles means that simply keeping the fleet on the road is itself a massive task.

The single most important factor keeping the Stobart army on the road is the team of diligent planners scattered around the country. William and Andrew have embraced technology since taking over the firm and a visit to the planning office in Carlisle is like entering a spaceship. A large open-plan room contains scores of planners, all studying computer screens and trying to organise their drivers as efficiently as possible. Each planner has many drivers who they are responsible for and it is a very demanding job.

Above: *William in one of Stobart's state-of-the-art planning centres.*

The company has around 350 planners, team leaders and managers connected to planning, strategically placed across four main centres, Carlisle, Appleton, Crick and Sherburn, plus a number of satellite depots. Lee Humphrey works as divisional planning manager at the Appleton depot and is hugely experienced in the demands of this particular role within the Stobart empire. He explains what the job entails: 'An order gets put through, either direct from the customer or manually created by our customer service team. This will have all the details that the planner and driver needs, such as the load details, collection and delivery times, what sort of job it is, such as whether it's a "drop and swap" job, all the info we need really.

'Each planner will have no more than 25 trampers, or a combination of 15 each of day/night drivers. We find that is a manageable amount to plan. It can be demanding, it's a challenging day but it doesn't usually overstretch them, otherwise they are not efficient. The planning side of the business has to be 24 hours, we have varying shift patterns to cope with the demand.'

Of course, 'best-laid plans' etc is a phrase that Lee knows only too well, as his staff's carefully plotted days can be turned on their heads at a moment's notice. With this job, expect the unexpected: 'Any number of things can happen to alter our best-laid plans. Traffic is the most obvious problem, so we have technology to feed news of problem spots through, we have a conference call three times a day with the planning managers to sift through all the traffic issues, we also have an instant traffic feed that gets sent out, and that helps us reorganise what we are planning. The weather is a big factor too – and not just bad weather such as snow, ice, wind, but if it's really hot there are more day-trippers or holidaymakers out on the road network.' Perhaps not surprisingly, Lee cites the winter snowstorms in the first week of December 2010 as the most challenging time of his planning career.

I ask Lee if it helps being a driver first, before going into planning, as a number of trampers had suggested: 'I think being a driver before becoming a planner has advantages as well as disadvantages. If you've been a driver, you have that knowledge of what the network is like out there, what certain drops are like, it's really useful; but then again, if you haven't been a driver you can sometimes bring a fresh pair of eyes to a situation, which can also be an advantage. For me, to have both sides of that in the planning office is key, it's crucial.'

There can be tension between drivers and planners at times: 'It's not a job without challenges, especially in terms of us asking drivers to do things they don't want to. But a lot of that goes down to how you approach it, how you talk to people, how you put the request across. At the end of the day, we have to remember we are all human beings.'

At the same time, some planners and drivers have very long and close professional relationships. Biomass driver Tim Fox speaks very highly of his planner: 'My planner Mike Borthwick is brilliant, he trusts me to do the work and I do it. Some planners think it's a remote-control truck and always phone you, but my planner gives me that freedom. I've had the same planner for years now. He even knows where most of the farms I have to find are, and some of them are in the middle of nowhere! You get to know your planner and how he works and he gets to know how you work. If your planner is an ex-driver it helps, because they know what you are doing. They know if what they are asking is possible, rather than, "The system says you can do this".'

The last word should go to Lee, who neatly sums up how the only certain thing about a planner's day is that nothing will be certain: 'You need to be quick on your toes, thinking all the time, because plans are constantly changing. It's not just delays, drivers sometimes get tipped quicker than you expect, that can also have a knock-on effect on your plans, so it's constantly shifting. Nothing ever stays the same.'

CRICK MAINTENANCE GARAGE

The Stobart fleet needs constant monitoring to keep the vehicles in tip-top condition. At the company's Crick depot, there is a team of eight mechanics working 24/7 in two specially designed garages at the Vehicle Maintenance Unit. The average truck replaces its tyres every year, at £250 each; with eight wheels on most trucks this can mean around 40,000–50,000 tyre changes a year (at any given moment, there are 1,800 trucks on the road as well as various other vehicles, which means some 37,000 tyres are in use). Fleet vehicles are also serviced every nine weeks.

Aside from standard repairs and upgrades to more than two thousand vehicles, the team also prepare the trucks for 5,500 MOTs per annum too, and their standards are so high that the company proudly maintains a 99 per cent pass rate. The number of tests and checks for an MOT on a HGV is exhaustive, with five hundred being needed just for the electrics. Typically there are around 850 maintenance incidents each month; the firm spends over £21,000 per month on repairs to curtains alone. This sort of meticulous eye for detail doesn't come cheap – Stobart spends over £13 million a year just maintaining the fleet.

There are other less obvious areas where Stobart need to keep the fleet running. In a snowy winter, they spend £20,000 a week clearing the depots, getting through 20 tonnes of road salt a day. If a single Stobart truck is stranded for a week, the company loses at least £500.

FUEL TANKERS

In a modern economy where fuel prices are constantly rising, spare a thought for Stobart the next time you curse at the petrol station. Every day they wake up to their trucks driving 500,000 miles in 24 hours, which is about 24 times around the earth; when you next

complain about your family car 'only' getting perhaps 30mpg, think of the fact that most trucks typically only manage around 8mpg. When the fleet is driving the equivalent of a trip to the moon and back every day, that's a lot of diesel.

That means that each year Stobart trucks travel over 180 million miles (to the sun and back) which means the company spends around £100 million on 97 million litres of diesel. That's a third of the company's entire running costs. If the price of diesel increases by just one penny a litre, Stobart are looking at an annual increase in their fuel bill of nearly £1 million.

With this colossal overhead in mind, Stobart have bought five of their own fuel tankers, specifically intended to keep the massive fleet fuelled up as economically as possible (two MAN trucks and three Scanias, with a further five Scanias on order). These MAN trucks cost £150,000 each and are capable of carrying 9,400 gallons of petrol or 8,000 gallons of heavier diesel. The orange plate on the front of the truck signifies it is carrying hazardous goods.

The fuel tankers come complete with six different internal compartments so that different types of fuel can be carried if required. Their six hoses stretch to 55

//STAT

A STANDARD STOBART TRAILER CAN CARRY AROUND 125,000 EMPTY DRINKS CANS.

feet in length and can discharge the entire tank of diesel in a matter of minutes (which, in such a time-pressured business as logistics, is itself an advantage).

Each driver is given a fuel card to pay for and monitor their usage. Using their own tankers generates a saving of around £4 per truck per refuel, which on the surface actually appears quite meagre. However, due to the sheer scale of the Stobart fleet, this equates to an annual saving of around £500,000. The Carlisle depot alone uses 55,000 gallons a week. The fuel tankers have proved to be such a hit that Stobart now even deliver fuel to rival haulage firms too!

There is a downside to this efficiency. Driving these trucks can be extremely hazardous. If the 8,000-gallon tanker were to be involved in an accident, the consequences could potentially be horrendous and almost certainly fatal to the driver and other road users, especially if the tank itself were punctured and exploded. Even though diesel is less unstable than unleaded petrol, the risk is still great. So there are only a handful of drivers at Stobart who are qualified to drive these trucks, and even then that is only after an additional six months of rigorous specialist training. Each time a truck collects or drops a tanker of fuel there are strenuous safety checks and the strictest procedures put in place by both the law and Stobart themselves. One additional demand is that once the truck is filled up and on the road, the driver has to compensate for the thousands of gallons of fuel swilling around behind him by driving with extra caution. The fuel can quite literally tip the tanker from side to side. It's not a job for the faint-hearted.

WASHING THE TRUCKS

'Apart from reliability, the most important feature of a Stobart truck is its appearance.' *Stobart Express* magazine, summer 1997.

In years gone by, first Edward and then William would obsessively clean their own trucks. As we have learned, long after the drivers had returned home, the two brothers could usually be found washing down the trucks ready for the next day. This attention to cleanliness is one of the central features of the Stobart success story.

However, no matter how enthusiastic they were with the sponge and bucket, it has been a long time since the two brothers could keep up the personal touch! After buying the £22,000 Karcher in the mid-1970s, the fleet kept growing and so too did the cost and effort involved in keeping the lorries clean.

Despite this, William and Edward have always insisted that their entire fleet is never anything other than spotless. To achieve this, the company has 13 truck-washing machines which wash a total of around 170 trucks each and every day around the UK.

The drivers have a choice of either a seven-minute speed wash if they are in a hurry or, if there is time, the luxury option, a full 23-minute gantry wash which is the Stobart truck's equivalent of an hour in a health spa. This superior wash uses 180 gallons of water (later recycled) per truck, and consists of a hand wash to begin with, then a chemical powered gantry wash which includes an in-built wax. Each superior wash costs Eddie Stobart £8. If every truck opts for that in a day, that's another £1,344 spent. Each year Stobart spend over £500,000 washing their trucks.

Tramper Mark Dixon is famous for his cleanliness: 'William likes things clean and tidy, he's famous for that, just look at our depots, they are all immaculately landscaped and presented. But I'm not gonna deny it, I think I've got OCD when

Above: *Another Stobart truck gets the full-wash treatment: even with the huge scale of the modern fleet, a lack of cleanliness is not tolerated by the company.*

THERE IS A SPECIAL RETURNS DEPOT AT CRICK TO HANDLE SO-CALLED 'SHOT LOADS' (ALONG WITH OTHER LOADS THAT CAN BE REJECTED FOR A VARIETY OF REASONS) WHICH CAN NUMBER AS HIGH AS 500 PALLETS A DAY. THAT MIGHT SOUND LIKE A FAIR NUMBER BUT THE COMPANY CAN DELIVER UP TO 26 MILLION PALLETS PER YEAR. AND SOMETIMES THE 'DAMAGE' IS HIGHLY SUBJECTIVE — A CUSTOMER ONCE REJECTED A PALLET BECAUSE THERE WAS ONE FLY INSIDE THE SHRINK-WRAP.

it comes to my truck. If it's dirty I don't want to drive it. If there are puddles, I will try to drive around them. You wouldn't get sacked if your truck was filthy, but they would say to you, "Why is your truck dirty?" There are washing bays all over our depots, so there's no excuse really. And I do it because I love to have a spotless, immaculate truck. I don't do it because I have to, I just love seeing Phoebe Grace sparkling.'

Mark is right – over the years William's attention to tiny detail has attained legendary status, quite possibly also verging on OCD! When he attends an office, someone will check that the window blinds are all straight first, that there are no coats on the backs of chairs and that everything is lined up correctly as it should be. William's son (also called Edward) even said his dad likes to line up his cans of food at home in an exact line. 'Always leave the stackyard tidy,' as Eddie Stobart himself used to say.

SAYING GOODBYE TO THE GIRLS

Each Stobart truck typically covers around 100,000-120,000 miles each year. By the end of year three, the company prefer to sell the lorries on, which helps to keep their fleet in tip-top condition and also helps to mitigate the huge annual bill of £55 million for buying 750 new lorries. The company would hope to sell a £70,000 truck with 350,000 miles on the clock for around £35,000. The money is welcome – Stobart have at times put seven new trucks a day on the road, which after a week would set them back over £500,000.

William Stobart often personally oversees the sales of the second-hand trucks and his famously fastidious eye for detail means the used lorries rarely leave the warehouse in anything other than near-perfect condition. Before leaving to a new home, each truck has the diesel siphoned off until the tank is around a quarter full: around 150 litres. Also, the famous Stobart livery has to be removed, which is done by steaming and peeling the vinyl wrap off, a painstaking process. Sadly,

VINYL WRAP

Since the introduction of vinyl wraps to the trucks in 2005, the fleet of Eddie Stobart vehicles has been one of the most modern and easy-to-spot haulage firms on the road. Each truck arrives plain white and is then sent to a specialist company for wrapping in the famous colours. For a Volvo truck there are 20 sections of vinyl which need to be attached using special magnets, after which the vinyl panels are baked on using a heat gun, which shrinks the material to the exact contours of the lorry. Any air bubbles or blemishes must be painstakingly weeded-out; otherwise, the wrap is abandoned and started again from scratch. There is a team of twelve men who can wrap eight trucks a day; each truck takes seven to eight hours.

along with the discarded vinyl, the truck's female name also dies with the truck. If a truck isn't sold, it might be used for much shorter, local drops, but the main aim is to move old vehicles on. The biomass driver I spent a day with, Tim Fox, thinks that Stobart's insistence on constantly updating their fleet has helped them keep one step ahead of the competition. 'They always give you decent kit. The wagons are changed every three years or so, they are quality trucks. They sell them on, but I'd rather work for the firm selling on a three-year-old truck than the one buying that second-hand wagon in.'

TRAILERS

While trampers in particular covet their trucks as their own, and have regularly been known to become emotional when their lorries are decommissioned, the trusty trailers attached to the backs of the cabs are not so affectionately regarded. They are shunted around the depots of the UK and Europe, swapping trucks frequently and being generally treated as the metallic workhorses that they are.

Stobart have around 35 different types of trailers, the most common being the curtain-siders that account for around 75 per cent of the fleet. They also own 500 rear-opening refrigerated trailers for the chilled division, 70 chipliners for the Biomass boys, 50 walking-floor trailers and 80 drawbars (which are used for high-volume, bulky loads).

At the Mansfield site of the trailer supplier SDC, more than 500 trailers are made each year. Each trailer costs about £25,000 and sees 24 workmen fit 37 separate components – such as ready-made doors, a roof and the curtains – on to a 'skeleton' base. Each trailer takes around two days to complete and the factory has the capacity to produce up to 50 each week at full tilt. Mansfield also upgrades trailers to higher specs and maintains older ones to a high standard. Before joining the fleet, any new trailer is first rigorously road tested. They are generally expected to last around five years. //

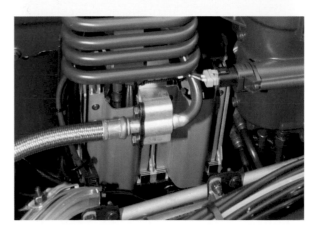

A mechanic's eye-view of a Scania R440 – underside and under the bonnet. A glorious spectacle of pipes, wires, cylinders and axles. Eddie Stobart trucks are almost constantly on the road, and need to be in top condition to ensure reliable delivery times for clients. The trucks are serviced every nine weeks, and the dedicated Stobart breakdown team is on call 24 hours, to repair any mechanical problems encountered on the road as quickly as possible.

Driving into the Future

EDDIE STOBART IS — BOTH METAPHORICALLY AND LITERALLY — CONSTANTLY ON THE MOVE. THIS INSTINCT TO PUSH FORWARD STARTED WAY BACK ON THAT CUMBRIAN FARM WITH EDDIE HIMSELF, BEFORE HIS SONS TOOK OVER THE MANTLE AND INJECTED THE FIRM WITH THEIR OWN INDIVIDUAL VISION. IN SOME WAYS, ALL THESE YEARS LATER, THE COMPANY HAS ONLY JUST STARTED ...

Since 2004, the massive expansion of Eddie Stobart into the multi-layered international logistics company it has become has been a remarkable new chapter in the firm's already unique history. However, the majority of the business still revolves around trucking. Fortunately, interest in being an Eddie Stobart driver extends beyond the musicians in the Wurzels. Given that the average age of the drivers is 46, with only five per cent under 30, Stobart is proactively seeking new blood, aware that the firm's longevity and competitiveness depend on being able to find and recruit a new generation of drivers. Each year, the company is swamped with interest from aspiring truck drivers, all keen to don the famous green shirt of the Stobart workforce; however, finding a new generation of drivers capable of meeting Stobart's high standards of life on the road is not always easy.

Above: *Building up driving skills on the Stobart truck simulator.*

For the younger, unqualified hopefuls, there is a prestigious logistics apprenticeship, which was started in 2007; the first person to graduate was Scott Macskimming in May of that year. The scheme is available to anyone with a clean driving licence and is based at the Stobart Training Academy in Widnes (opened in 2011) which greets a total of 150 hopefuls each year. With the current cost of a HGV licence being in the region of £3,000, apprenticeships such as this are a precious chance for young people to land the job of a lifetime.

The first two weeks see the recruits put through their paces in an intensive course where they learn about the trucks, the road regulations and driving skills required. Eventually they will take their HGV2 licence test, now known as 'Class C', which costs £1,000 and only allows them to drive rigid trucks. They also have to shadow their 'mentor' drivers on actual drops, where they can learn all about the challenges and pitfalls of being a Stobart driver.

One of the gadgets that is used by the hopefuls is the Eddie Stobart truck simulator. This costs in the region of £250,000 and replicates in precise detail what it is like to drive a full-size truck. It comes complete with an adjustable air-pressured seat, a 16-speed gearbox, six rear-view mirrors and a full dashboard interior. Virtual 'roads' are projected onto a two-metre wide screen and the computer system is equipped with 120 miles of roads across various types of terrain, including mountain tracks.

Once the HGV2 licence is acquired, the trainees start learning the considerably greater skills that are required for them to achieve a full HGV Class 1 pass.

To successfully complete the intensive apprenticeship takes a gruelling six months.

The academy also keeps up the standards of Stobart's already qualified drivers, with refresher courses and updates on the latest legal requirements of their job. These periodic refresher courses are complemented by drivers being trained to NVQ Level 2 in Driving Goods Vehicles. To date, 1,200 Stobart drivers have been trained. The new qualification demonstrates driver competence; every driver entered to date has passed.

Above: *An instructor addresses lucky apprentices at the Widnes Training Academy.*

Even for those already holding an HGV1, competition for work is still fierce. In 2011, Stobart launched a massive recruitment drive to find 600 new drivers – yet over 8,000 people applied! There is also a respected driver-training school at Crick consisting of 20 trainers and support staff. Seven trainers are DSA-registered LGV instructors.

Sometimes the positions are temporary to meet exceptional demand. For example, Christmas is the busiest period for the whole fleet because the nation wants its festive food. During this time, Stobart trucks drive the equivalent of 40 times around the Earth each day, delivering four million turkeys, picking up 25,000 Christmas trees every 24 hours (you can fit around 2,000 in one curtain-sider), and delivering 9,000 times a day. To meet demand, Stobart add 500 temporary trucks to their fleet.

NEW VOLVO FH16

Both Edward and William Stobart have prided themselves on their adoption of new technology and their firm will always be first in the queue to try new trucks, trailers or other innovations. Viewers of the TV show *Trucks & Trailers* will be familiar with the arrival of one such new star on the Stobart fleet: the £170,000 Volvo FH16. This is one of the most powerful trucks on Britain's roads, with a 700bhp engine (compared to the standard truck's 460bhp) that can reach speeds of around 90mph if unrestricted. This colossal power is equivalent to top-of-the-range Ferraris or Lamborghinis and means the truck could in theory pull seven double-deckers up a hill at 56mph!

Inside the cab, the gadgets include a lane-control detector, active cruise control and a brand new 'blindspot alarm' which alerts the driver to any person, vehicle or obstacle in the danger zone. The cab itself is upholstered in leather – including on the steering wheel.

One of Stobart most popular drivers, tramper Matt Ekin, was given the honour of taking this truck to Stobart's big 40th anniversary bash at London's Battersea Power Station. The lorry was to be the centrepiece of the gala night, which made it all the more excruciating when Matt – widely regarded as one of Stobart's finest drivers and a proudly loyal employee – became snarled up in impossible London streets and scraped the FH16's rear bumper on the front wing of a parked car, in full view of the cameras. Fortunately the damage was minimal and overnight the scratched bumper was replaced, so that the new Volvo was flawless when it was stationed in its very own white marquee for the party night.

A Final
Word

With a rich heritage behind them and a bright future to look forward to, the road ahead is certain to be as eventful for Eddie Stobart as the company's colourful and indeed unique past.

The tale of Eddie Stobart is in many ways the tale of a modern celebrity: a working-class boy 'done good', a business that through sheer graft, ingenuity and ambition ensured that its name became firmly embedded in the public consciousness. The Stobart family has redefined an industry. Ask most people to name a haulage firm and there's usually only one man's name that crops up. Stobart's own company biography is also emblematic of a wider narrative: the story of how the haulage firms whose trucks we see ploughing up and down our roads are complex, demanding and difficult businesses to run. The hours are long, the customers are at times unforgiving, and uncontrollable circumstances can conspire against them every day. Each of the many thousands of drivers sitting in those famous liveried trucks have their own stories, too; personal tales of how they came to be HGV drivers and also tales from the road, both good and bad.

Above: *The new Volvo FH16 out on a delivery in the Stobart heartlands, the Peak District countryside.*

It's also the story of constant advances in technology, from trucks with wooden cabs to state-of-the-art articulated lorries with on-board computers and GPS systems. It's the story of millions of pallets a year being picked up and dropped off, of unusual loads being delivered and impossible deadlines being met. And it's a story that's had more twists and turns than any winding A-road you may care to mention.

And yet it's not actually the number of trucks, the size of the warehouses, the millions of pallets or the staggering logistical complexities of running this monstrously huge fleet that linger in the mind. Perhaps it is the people at the heart of this family haulage firm who can recount the most remarkable journeys in this book. Stobart is an iconic brand founded on personalities.

The three distinct phases of the Eddie Stobart story have each been so crucial: Eddie himself with all his teenage entrepreneurial energy and determination to set up a business, look after his family and yet always hold his faith dear; his son Edward, who grabbed a small family firm and turned it into a haulage icon through vision, hard work and unerring self-belief; and finally his younger brother William and best friend Andrew Tinkler, whose takeover in 2004 was potentially fraught with difficulties yet has been remarkable for the exponential growth, diversification and profitability they have returned to the company.

When asked about his dad, Eddie Stobart, William explains that his father is really happy with the success of the family firm but is equally happy to have left the stage when he did. 'He's fine with it, he wasn't involved from such an early point... I can remember me dad working but very vaguely, from when I was 18 onwards he was a gardener, mostly! It's a very modern business and I don't think he's been really that interested, to a certain extent. All those trucks have got his name down the side of course, but he had his faith and his own business and he was completely content with that.'

Sadly we cannot ask Edward to reflect on the massive success he created but instead have to look back to the typically phlegmatic and modest words he spoke in the 1990s: 'We never turn any customer away and we always do it at the right price. We are always smart, tidy – the best at everything. We have the smartest drivers and the smartest trucks and we do our job well, which is why people notice us and why we are a success.'

As for William – who has been there from the very beginning, washing trucks, driving them, repairing them, working in the office, rising to executive level and eventually buying the entire company with his friend, Andrew Tinkler, – his surname is a bold reminder of what is in essence the triumph of an entire family. William is the beating heart of the company and is rightly very proud of what he and Andrew have achieved in a relatively short period of time. The youngest of the Stobart children grew up surrounded by trucks, tractors, machinery and a business that has transformed the Stobart family's legacy. I ask him which part of his massive, complex and multi-faceted empire he enjoys the most: 'I still love the transport side, I was born and bred there. I love the customer side, pricing work, getting work, the planning element of it, I still love that. It's back to basics, I guess.'

When I ask him if he has any regrets, William ponders for a moment then a sparkle flashes behind his eyes as he recalls a cherished memory. As he speaks up, there is a glimpse across his face of the young boy sitting on the farm wall back in the 1960s, waiting for some gnarly old driver to pull up in his beloved truck, wind down the window and shout, 'Do you want to come out, boy?'

'I miss tramping, I know that sounds funny but I still miss it. I've got a farm and I sell horse shavings, it's just a little business on the side and for that I've got an artic and a good lad who delivers for me. I find that very relaxing… and I spend every Saturday morning washing the truck.' //

Fleet List/

NAMED VEHICLES ON THE ROAD IN AUGUST 2012

Abbey Lou	Alison	Amy Everest	Anneliese Helene	Becky Rachel
Abbie Catherine	Alison Claire	Amy Jayne	Annetta Veronica	Bella
Abbie Catherine	Alison Eileen	Amy Jayne	Annette	Bertha Ellen
Abbie Faye	Alison Eileen	Amy Leigh	Annette Kim	Bertie
Abby Louise	Alison Jane	Amy Marie	Annie Elizabeth	Beryl
Abi	Alison Jean	Amy Michelle	Anthea Caroline	Beryl Ann
Abigail Amanda	Alison Joanne	Amy Norah	Anthea Margaret	Beryl Marjorie
Abigail Jane	Alison Sarah	Amy Susanna	Anya Elizabeth	Beryl Vera
Abigail Natassia	Aliyah Grace	Amy Victoria	Anysia Rose	Beth Ann
Adele Grace	Ally	Amy Violet	April Louise	Beth Avril
Adele Janene	Ally Ann	Anastasia Lisa	Arianna	Beth Elin
Adele Louise	Ally Nikki	Andrea Lily	Arianne Elise	Bethan Ffion
Adele Rowena	Allyssa Sammie	Andrea Louise	Arianne Elsie	Bethany Anne
Adria Lynn	Amanada Lorraine	Angel	Ashlea Victoria	Bethany Charlette
Ady Jayne	Amanda Mary	Angela	Ashlee Ann	Bethany Denise
Aimee	Amanda Milly	Angela Mary	Ashleigh Elizabeth	Bethany Georgina
Aimee	Amanda Rebecca	Angela May	Ashleigh Jade	Bethia Miriam
Aimee Bella	Amanda Theresa	Angharad Kristina	Audra Ann	Bettina
Aimee Callie	Amber Grace	Angie Annie	Audrey	Beverley Judith
Aimee Mae	Amber Jane	Angie Lauren	Audrey Ann	Bianca Elizabeth
Aimee Morven	Amber Jessica	Anita	Audrey Sonia	Bisola Toni
Alana	Amberlee Susan	Anita Mary	Autumn Rose	Bobby
Alanah Maria	Amelia	Anita Merle	Ava Blossom	Bonnie Belle
Alara Elle	Amelia	Ann Ballentine	Ava Maria	Brenda
Alex Alicia	Amelia Charlotte	Ann Cynthia	Ava May	Brenda Joyce
Alex Jo	Amelia Coco	Ann Elizabeth	Ava Minnie	Brenny
Alexa Jayne	Amelia Dorothy	Ann Georgina	Ava Rose	Bridged Elizabeth
Alexandra Christine	Amelia Ella	Ann Irene	Avice Hilary	Bridie Marina
Alexandra Grace	Amelia Grace	Ann Patrica	Avis Elise	Bromwyn Levaine
Alexandra Jane	Amelia Joy	Ann Patricia	Avis Elsie	Bronte Laura
Alexandra Nia	Amelia Rehiannon	Anna	Barbara	Bronwen
Alexandria 21	Amelia Rose	Anna Charlotte	Barbara Ann	Bronwen Bella
Alexia Mae	Amelia Rose	Anna Emma	Barbara Anne	Bryony Leander
Alexia Phoebe	Amelie Emma	Anna Jane	Barbara Christine	Cairo Louise
Alexis Bernadette	Amelie Layla	Anna Kate	Barbara Cristina	Caitlin Dellen
Alice Ann	Amelie Violet	Annabel Jane	Barbara Elizabeth	Caitlin Eve
Alice Elizabeth	Ami Jane	Annabel Paige	Barbara Kay	Caitlin May
Alice Emily	Amy	Annalies Sophia	Barbara Ruth	Caitlyn Liann
Alice Grace	Amy Annie	Anne	Beatrice Ann	Calissia Rose
Alice Louise	Amy Beth	Anne	Beatrice Joyce	Calista Madison
Alice Megan	Amy Bethany	Anne Christine	Beatrice May	Callie Rose
Alicia Jayne	Amy Claire	Anne Marie	Beatrix	Cara Sorcha
Aline Elizabeth	Amy Ellen	Anne Maureen	Beatrix Ella	Carey Louise
Alisha Maye	Amy Emily	Anneliese Fleur	Becci Tracy	Carissa Annie

Carla Marie
Carlene Leona
Carly
Carly Frances
Carmon Eileen
Carol Ann
Carol Ann
Carol Elizabeth
Carol Elizabeth
Carol Jo
Carole
Carole Bess
Carole Evelyn
Carole Lillian
Carole Lynn
Caroline
Caroline Jane
Caroline Joanne
Caroline Rachel
Carys Louise
Casey Nicole
Catalina Marie
Catherine Amy
Catherine Bernadette
Catherine Claire
Catherine Florence
Catherine Laura
Catherine Louise
Catherine Margaret
Catherine Mary
Catherine Mary
Catherine Sophia
Catherine Susan
Cathrine Ann
Cathy Anne
Catrin Angharad
Catrina
Catrina Elizabeth
Catrina Petra
Catriona Grace
Catriona Laura
Catriona Mary
Cayla Louise
Cerys Aimie
Cerys Theodora
Cesca Olivia

Chantal Emmeline
Chantelle
Chantelle Danielle
Chantelle Elizabeth
Chantelle Lauren
Chantelle Sophie
Charis Anne
Charlee Cerys
Charley Diane
Charley Rose
Charlie Jade
Charlie Simone
Charlotte
Charlotte June
Charlotte Darcy
Charlotte Ellie
Charlotte Elyse
Charlotte Francesca
Charlotte Jane
Charlotte Karla Alexandra
Charlotte Kate
Charlotte Kathleen
Charlotte Lindsay
Charlotte Louise
Charlotte Mae
Charlotte Marion
Charlotte Rebecca
Charlotte Rose
Charlotte Sofia
Charlotte Suzanne
Chelsea Jade
Cheri Jayne
Cherri Louise
Cheryl
Cheryl
Cheryl Irene
Cheryl Leah
Cheryl Lindsay
Cheyenne Louise
Chloe
Chloe Beth
Chloe Chelsie
Chloe Denise
Chloe France
Chloe Jade
Chloe Jane

Chloe Jenny
Chloe Jo
Chloe Leigh
Chloe Natalie
Christina Beth
Christina Corinne
Christina Louise
Christine Claire
Christine Elizabeth
Christine Ellen
Christine Eve
Christine Ruth
Ciara Leigh
Ciara Roxy
Cindy Lou
Claire
Claire Amanda
Claire Elizabeth
Claire Elizabeth
Claire Emma
Claire Louise
Claire Louise
Clare Geraldine
Claudette Lucy
Claudia Charlotte
Cleo Elizabeth
Cleo Lola
Codey Wray
Colette Leigh
Colette Leigh
Collette Cheryl
Connie
Connie May
Corah Faye
Coral Madeline
Coralie
Corbie Jayne
Corine Olive
Corrina
Courtney Amy
Courtney Liana
Crissy
Crystal Charlie
Cyndy
Daisy
Daisy

Daisy Anna
Daisy Emma
Daisy Mae
Daisy Norina
Damson Madison
Danann
Danica
Danica Jade
Daniella
Danielle Louise
Danielle Marie
Danyela
Daphne May
Darcey Erin
Darci Victoria
Darcy Elizabeth
Darcy Grace
Daryll Anne
Dawn Elizabeth
Dawn Francis
Dawn Marie
Dawn Marie
Dawnie
Dayna Marie
Deanna Patricia
Debbie Alex
Debbie Ann
Debbie Laura
Debbie Lynne
Debbie Marjorie
Debby
Deborah Channon
Deborah Jane
Deborah Louise
Dee
Delphine Annette
Delyth Mary
Demi
Demi Jai
Demi Jo
Demi Leigh
Denna Elizabeth
Destiny Amelie
Destiny Anais
Destiny Leigh
Devon Katie

Diane Helen
Diane Sylvia
Dominique Stacey
Donella Mary
Donna Marie
Donna Michelle
Dora
Doreen Elizabeth
Doreen Mary
Dorinda Elizabeth
Doris Mavis
Doris May
Doris May
Doris Rose
Dorothy
Dorothy Catherine
Dorothy Laura
Dorothy Vera
Drew
Ebony Pamela
Eden Elizabeth
Edith Danni
Edith Mary
Edith May
Eileen Ruth
Eileen Theresa
Eilidh Rose
Eilish Charlotte
Eilish Kathleen
Elaine Alexandra
Elaine Catherine
Elaine Margaret
Eleanor Caroline
Eleanor Hannah
Eleanor Liberty
Eleanor May
Eleanor Rose
Elena
Elena Carina
Eleni Elizabeth
Elfie
Elise Catherine
Elisha Jade
Elisha Marie
Elissa Brooke
Eliza Scarlett

Elizabeth Agnes	Emily Harriet	Evie Estelle	Gail Julia	Gladys Duchess Of Overton
Elizabeth Georgia	Emily Jane	Evie Francesa	Gallega	Glenda
Elizabeth Hilary	Emily Jane	Evie Jane	Gallega	Glenda Lucille
Elizabeth Jean	Emily Jayne	Evie Louise	Gallega	Glenice
Elizabeth Mary	Emily June	Evie May	Gaynor Isabella	Glennis Rosemary
Elizabeth Mavis	Emily Kate	Evie Rose	Gaynor Lorraine	Glynis Wendy
Elizabeth Paula	Emily Lauren	Evie Sophia	Gem Gems	Grace Alice
Elizabeth Phyllis	Emily Louisa	Evie Sophia	Gemma Charlotte	Grace Elizabeth
Ella Bella	Emily Mae	Evora Scarlet	Gemma Elizabeth	Grace Elizabeth
Ella Emily	Emily Margaret	Evora Scarlet	Gemma Elizabeth	Grace Elizabeth
Ella India	Emily Olivia	Fay Emily	Gemma Kate	Grace Harriet
Ella India	Emily Sue	Feena Jean	Gemma Kate	Grace Leah
Ella Louise	Emma	Felicity Jane	Gemma Lauren	Grace Nicole
Ella Sharon	Emma Alexandra	Felicity Louise	Gemma Lou	Grace Olivia
Elle Anne	Emma Ann	Felisha Fay	Gemma Louise	Grace Rebekah
Elle Dixie	Emma Brenda	Fiona Helen	Gemma Lucy	Grace Rebekah
Elle Mae	Emma Carmel	Fiona Lynne	Genevieve	Grace Ruby
Ellen Jane	Emma Catriney	Fiona Mary	Georgia Allison	Grace Teresa
Ellena	Emma Jade	Fiona Valerie	Georgia Chloe	Gracie May
Ellexie Grace	Emma Jo Violet	Flo	Georgia Daisy	Gracie Rose
Ellie Abby	Emma Joan	Flo	Georgia Elizabeth	Gracie Rose
Ellie Jai	Emma Mary	Flo Jo	Georgia Elly	Gwendoline Anne
Ellie Jane	Emma Ruby	Florence Emily	Georgia Faye	Gwendoline Margaret
Ellie Jean	Emma Victoria	Florence Lilian	Georgia Grace	Gwyneira Gwyther
Ellie Joanne	Emma Wynne	Frances Annie	Georgia Maddison	Gwyneth Joy
Ellie Lauren	Enid Irene	Frances Elizabeth	Georgia Nicole	Hafryn
Ellie Louise	Erica Jane	Frances Mary	Georgia Rose	Haifa Mary
Ellie Mae	Erica Mae Stacey	Francine Julia	Georgie Collett	Halle Jacqueline
Ellie May	Erin Grace	Frankie	Georgina	Hana Jane
Ellie Rose	Erinn Mary	Frankie Jorgia	Georgina Chrissy	Hanna Marie
Ellie Sophie	Esme Emily	Frankie Sylvia	Georgina Helen	Hannah Amy
Ellis Olivia	Esme Jane	Freda	Georgina Henrietta	Hannah Dilys
Ellis Rebekah	Esmee Louise	Freda Bernice	Georgina Iris	Hannah Frankie
Eloise Eve	Esther Elisabeth	Freya Ann	Georgina Jamie	Hannah Grace
Elsie	Esther Nora	Freya Grace	Geraldine	Hannah Jade
Elsie Faith	Esther Robina	Freya Lily	Gertrude Belle	Hannah Jane
Elsie Marjorie	Ethel May	Freya May	Gertrude Rachel	Hannah Kate
Emilia & Bella	Eva Joyce	Freya Mccalla	Gill	Hannah Kate
Emilia Grace	Eva Mya	Freya Poppy	Gillian Ann	Hannah Louise
Emilia Jane	Eve Ellen	Gabriella Charlotte	Gillian Elizabeth	Hannah Michelle
Emilia Lily	Eve Lauren	Gabrielle Jo	Gillian Katheryn	Hannah Sian
Emily	Evelyn Daisy	Gabrielle Lily	Gillian Margaret	Harley
Emily Ann	Evelyn Josephine	Gabrielle Lily	Gillian Mary	Harriet Freya
Emily Caroline	Evelyn Mary	Gail	Gillian Susan	Harriet Grace
Emily Christina	Evie	Gail Elizabeth	Gillie Krystal	Harriet Louise
Emily Clare	Evie Alice	Gail Elizabeth	Gilly Joey	Harriet Nicole

Hayley
Hayley Lee
Hayley Louise
Hayley Michelle
Hazel Christine
Hazel Jill
Hazel Margaret
Hazel Rosina
Heather Eve
Heather Grace
Heather Jane
Heather Louise
Heather Mary
Heidi Elizabeth
Heidi Jo
Heidi Willow
Helen Alice
Helen Cecilia
Helen Chloe
Helen Elizabeth
Helen Margaret
Helen Marie
Helen Rachel
Helen Rebecca
Helen Stephanie
Helen Victoria
Helena
Helena Jane
Hermione Rose
Hilary Anne
Hilary Denise
Hilary Janet
Hilary Louise
Hollie Alana
Hollie Bailey
Hollie Hannah
Holly
Holly Belle
Holly Brooke
Holly Kate
Holly Lauren
Honey Margaret
Immarni Jade
Imogen Abbie
Imogen Anne
Imogen Emily

Ina Jane
India Mae
India Rose
Indiana Shakira
Indra
Inglis Drever
Iona Louise
Iona Rosalind
Irene Amanda
Irene Elizabeth
Irene Maud
Isabel Bernice
Isabela Scarlet
Isabella Darcey
Isabella Darcy
Isabella Helen
Isabella Kate
Isabella Rose
Isabella Victoria
Isabella Victoria
Isabelle Jane
Isabelle June
Isabelle Mary
Isabelle Nikki
Isabelle Rose
Isabelle Rose
Isabelle Victoria
Isla Alexa
Isla Bowe
Isla Isabella
Isla Rose
Isla Rose
Isobel
Isobel Grace
Isobel Joy
Isobel May
Ivana Helen
Ivy
Ivy Grace
Ivy Valentine
Izabela Aleksandra
Izzy Mae
Jac Anne
Jackie Yvonne
Jacqueline
Jacqueline Ann

Jacqueline Anne
Jacqueline Mary
Jacqueline Sarah
Jacualine Edwina
Jade Abby
Jade Amy
Jade Kathryn
Jade Mckenzie
Jade Samantha
Jaime Anne
Jaki Roberta
Jaki Roberta
Jamie Danielle
Jamie Megan
Jan
Jana Anna
Jane Elizabeth
Jane Emily
Jane Kathleen
Jane Marie
Jane Olivia
Janet Helen
Janet Marie
Janet Mary
Janet Susan
Janette Lynagh
Janice Christine
Janice Elizabeth
Janice Mary
Janice Rosemary
Janice Rosemary
Janina Mary
Janine
Janine Carol
Jasmine Christine
Jasmine Katie
Jasmine Nicole
Jasmine Veronica
Jay Jules
Jay Michelle
Jayne
Jayne Anne
Jean
Jean Ann
Jean Evelyn
Jean Margaret

Jean Mary
Jean Muriel
Jean Ursula
Jean Valarie
Jean Valerie
Jeanette Carol
Jeanette Catherine
Jeanette Sophia
Jeanne Colette
Jeanne Mary
Jeannie Lynn
Jennee Louise
Jenni Rebbeka
Jennifer Alison
Jennifer Angela
Jennifer Ann
Jennifer Elizabeth
Jennifer Helen
Jennifer Joy
Jennifer May
Jennifer Ruth
Jenny
Jenny Anne
Jessica
Jessica Abigail
Jessica Amelia
Jessica Amy
Jessica Amy
Jessica Caitlyn
Jessica Daisy
Jessica Ella
Jessica Jean
Jessica Jude
Jessica June
Jessica Leah Kylie
Jessica Leigh
Jessica Lily
Jessica Louise
Jessica Marie
Jessica Nicole
Jessica Patricia
Jessica Pheobe
Jessica Rose
Jessica Sophie Mae
Jessie Mae
Jessie Marguerite

Jill Adelaide
Jill Elizabeth
Jill Rebecca
Jillian Hazel
Jinette
Jinny Olivia
Jo
Jo Albertina
Joan Audrey
Joan Lillian
Joanna
Joanna Margaret
Joanna Polly
Joanne
Joanne Catherine
Joanne Hazel
Joanne Marie
Joanne Shiela
Joanne Sophia
Jodi Louise
Jodie Beth
Jodie Leah
Jodie Megan
Johannah Elizabeth
Jorja Paige
Josephine Clare
Josie Louise
Josie Marie
Joy
Joy Margaret
Joy Marry
Joyce Amy
Joyce Ann
Joyce Evelyn
Joyce Gem
Judith
Judith Anne
Judith Kaye
Judith Margaret
Judith Mary
Jules
Julia Amelia
Julia Anne
Julia Anne
Julia Lynn
Julia Mary

Julia Rose
Julia Susan
Julie
Julie Ann
Julie Caroline
Julie Claire
Julie Dawn
Julie Dawn
Julie Elaine
Julie Elaine
Julie Elizabeth
Julie Linda
Julieanne Libby
June Lesley
June Rosemary
Justine Sophie
Kacey Lousie
Kaileigh Rachel
Kaitlin Molly
Kalli Maia
Kara Faye
Karen Angela
Karen Anne
Karen Chelsey
Karen Dawn
Karen Diane
Karen Emma
Karen Joy
Karen Laura
Karen Lesley
Karen Michelle
Karen Patricia
Karin
Karrelle Emma
Katarzyna
Kate Amelia
Kate Jane
Kate Michelle
Katharina Jean
Katherine Ellen
Katherine Zarin
Kathie Helen
Kathie Helen
Kathleen Alison
Kathleen Christina
Kathleen Elizabeth

Kathleen Mavis
Kathleen Veronica
Kathrin
Kathryn Grace
Kathryn Jane
Kathryn Linda
Kathryn Marie
Kathryn Marie
Kathryn Mary
Katie Anne
Katie Chloe
Katie Jeorgina
Katie Leah
Katie Lilian
Katie Lou
Katie Louise
Katie Phoebe
Katie Rebecca
Katie Sophie
Katie Sue
Kay
Kay
Kay Diane
Kay Helen
Keeley Dakota
Keeley Rose
Kelly Alexa
Kelly Anne
Kelly Louisa
Kelly Mary
Kelly Michelle
Kelly Teresa
Kellyann
Kerima Ann
Kerra
Kerry Ann
Kerry Anne
Kerry Louise
Kerry Marie
Kerry Sarah
Kerry Suzanne
Kerryn
Kezia Ann
Kiah Lian
Kim Annette
Kim Lesley

Kim Lesley
Kim Louise
Kim Rachael
Kim Rackel
Kimberley
Kimberley Anne
Kimberley Elizabeth
Kimberley Jane
Kimberley Louise
Kimbley Jeannette
Kinzie
Kirsten Eve
Kirsten Kara
Kirsten Louise
Kirstie Louise
Kirstie Mary Ann
Kirsty Aileen
Kirsty Beth
Kirsty Jane
Kirsty Tina
Klarissa Paige
Kloeigh Madaline
Kodee Louise
Kristen May
Kristin Rianne
Krystal
Kylie Danika
Kyra
Lady Audrey
Lady Tracy
Lakota Skye
Lana Scarlett
Lara Michelle
Laura Abby
Laura Ann
Laura Ann
Laura Anne
Laura Ciara
Laura Dawn
Laura Gail
Laura Georgia
Laura Hanna
Laura Helen
Laura Iris
Laura Jade
Laura Jane

Laura Jayne
Laura Joanne
Laura Katharine
Laura Louise
Laura Louise
Laura Marie
Laura Mill
Laura Monique
Lauren Rebecca
Lauren Aimee
Lauren Ann
Lauren Chelsea
Lauren Elisabeth
Lauren Elizabeth
Lauren Jade Anna
Lauren Jane
Lauren Leigh
Lauren Lousie
Lauren Nicolle
Lauren Rachel
Lauren Rose
Lauren Sarah
Layla Karen
Leah Edana
Leah Faye
Leah Jane
Leah Jordan
Leah Victoria
Leanne Christina
Leanne Louise
Leigh Anne
Leigh Jayne
Leigh Margaret
Leila Rose
Leilah Jolene
Leisa Enlli
Leona Jade
Leona Jude
Leoni
Leoni Jordan
Leoni Louise
Leonie Kate
Leonie Megan
Leonie Tamsin
Leshka
Lesley

Lesley Eunice
Lettie Scarlette
Levina Darcy
Lexie Amelia
Lexie Keeva
Lexie Lou
Lexie Lou
Lianne Andrea
Lianne Faye
Libbie Lexie
Libby Kay
Libby Mae
Libby Mae
Libby Rose
Libby Summer
Liberty Samantha
Lilian Audrey
Lillian Mary
Lilly Ella
Lilly Jane
Lilly Mai
Lilly Rose
Lily Grace
Lily Kathleen
Lily Penelope
Lily Rebecca
Lily Rose
Lilymae
Linda
Linda
Linda
Linda Ann
Linda Christine
Linda Elizabeth
Linda Ellen
Linda Helen
Linda Margaret
Linda Rosemary
Linda Samantha
Linda Swan
Lindsay Moya
Linsey Christina
Liona Katrina
Lisa
Lisa Jayne
Lisa Olivia

Livia Darcie	Lucy Imogen	Mara Elizabeth	Maxine	Mikasa Gwendoline
Livvy Eve	Lucy Jane	Mara Jade	Maxine	Millicent Matilda
Lizzie Beth	Lucy Mai	Marcia Claudette	Maxine Anne	Millie Anne
Lizzie Maria	Lucy Mary	Margaret Doreen	Maxine Natalie	Millie Jo
Lois Ellen	Lucy May	Margaret Evelyn	Maxine Patricia	Millie Meghan
Lois Valentine	Lucy Poppy	Margaret Janet	Maxine Pearl	Millie Rose
Lola Christine	Lucy Rebecca	Margaret Rita	May Lou	Millie Tasha
Lola Marie	Lydia Corrinne	Margaret Vanessa	Maya Jemima	Milly Moo
Lola Mathilda	Lydia Grace	Margery Carys	Mayson Louise	Mindy Moo
Lola Seren	Lyn Alejandrino	Margery Elizabeth	Megan Alicia	Minnie Kathryn
Lola Teresa	Lyn Kathleen	Maria Bethan	Megan Elizabeth	Minnie Wynne
Loo-Ise	Lynda Dawn	Maria Jane	Megan Leigh	Moira Margaret
Loo-Ise	Lynda Jayne	Marian Lena	Megan Louise	Mollie Ann
Loraine Elizabeth	Lynda Jean	Marie Delores	Megan Mae	Mollie Rose
Lorna Ann	Lynda Joyce	Marie Therese	Megan Rose	Molly
Lorna Dawn	Lynda Mary	Marietta Celina	Meghan Elizabeth	Molly Ann
Lorna Jane	Lyndsay Anne	Marilyn Ann	Meghan Rose	Molly Anne
Lottie Jean	Lynette Angela	Marilyn Ann	Meiriona	Molly Casey
Louanne	Lynn	Marilyn Eva	Melanie Dawn	Molly Darcy
Louisa	Lynn Frances	Marina	Melanie Maureen	Molly Dolly
Louise Alexandra	Lynn Patricia	Marina Elizabeth	Melanie Rachael	Molly Kate
Louise Anne	Lynne Davina	Marine Elise	Melanie Ruth	Molly Rose
Louise Annette	Lynne Leigh	Marion Elizabeth	Melena Jane	Molly Victoria
Louise Elizabeth	Mabel Milly	Marion Netta	Melisa	Monica Trinity
Louise Isabella	Macey Lily	Marion Rose	Melissa	Mooneen Minnie
Louise Jayne	Macey Rhea	Marion Sadie	Melissa Nicole	Morgan Daisy
Louise Mary	Mackenzie Holly	Marjorie Doris	Meredith Jane	Morgan Ellis
Loyita Monica	Mackenzie Jade	Marjorie Joan	Merle	Morgan Heidi
Lucia Marcelle	Madalaine Rose	Marjorie Theresa	Merridith Laura	Morgan Leigh
Luciana Rose	Maddison Irene	Marlene Elizabeth	Mia Anne	Morgan Patricia
Lucie Megan	Maddison Pauline	Marnie Elsie	Mia Charlotte	Morgane Louise
Lucy	Madeleine Cefai	Martha	Mia Louise	Mozelle Elizabeth
Lucy Amber	Madison Poppy	Martha Rose	Mia Lousie	Muriel Jane
Lucy Brooke	Maegan Elise	Martha Susanna	Mia Rose	Muriel Peace
Lucy Caitlin	Magarita	Mary Amanda	Michaela	Muriel Rosa
Lucy Eleanor	Magda	Mary Ann	Michaela Jane	Nadine Bethany
Lucy Elizabeth	Maggie Ann	Mary Elizabeth	Michele Denise	Nancy Elizabeth
Lucy Elizabeth	Maggie May	Mary Josephine	Michelle Alma	Nancy May
Lucy Emma	Maisie	Mary Kathleen	Michelle Clare	Naomi
Lucy Georgia	Maisie Amelia	Mary Lou	Michelle Hannah	Naomi Chloe
Lucy Hannah	Maisie Jayne	Mary Mildred	Michelle Hawkes	Naomi Jade
Lucy Hannah	Mandie	Matilda Grace	Michelle Lorraine	Naomi Ruth
Lucy Hannah	Mandie Sam	Maureen Hilary	Michelle Louise	Natali Patricia
Lucy Hayley	Mandy	Maureen Pat	Michelle Louise	Natalie Alice
Lucy Heather	Mandy Ann	Mavis	Mikala Amie	Natalie Andrea
Lucy Helena	Mandy Jane	Mavis Cynthia	Mikala Michelle	Natalie Camilla

Natalie Claire
Natalie Jane
Natalie Lauren
Natalie Rhys
Natasha Siobhan
Nathasha Ann
Neave Elizabeth
Neish
Neisha Catherine
Nellie Ethel
Nellie Mai
Neola May
Nerys Mallene
Neve Anne
Neve Marie
Nevina Barbara
Niamh
Niamh Katy
Niamh Mary
Nichole Louise
Nicki Louise
Nicky Danielle
Nicola
Nicola Belle
Nicola Joanne
Nicola Kate
Nicola Marie
Nicola Marie
Nicole Clare
Niketa Christine
Nikita Michelle
Nikki Fae
Niko
Nikola Denise
Nina Jonet
Nina Pamela
Nora Mable
Norah Bernadette
Norah Margaret
Noranne
Norma
Norma Kerry
Ocean Leigh
Odette Savannah
Olave St Claire
Olive Margaret

Olivia
Olivia Charlotte
Olivia Claire
Olivia Edie
Olivia Eve
Olivia Faye
Olivia G
Olivia Grace
Olivia Grace
Olivia Iris
Olivia Keturah
Olivia Louise
Olivia Rose
Olivia Susan
Olivia Susan
Olivia Suzanne
Oonagh
Oriel Cicley
Orla Grace
Orlaith Jude
Paige Alice
Paige Ann
Paige Ann
Paige Emma
Paighton Lee
Pamela Ann
Pamela Eileen
Pamela Jane
Pamela Jean
Pamela Joyce
Pamela Julie
Pandora Emily
Paris Rio
Pat Kerry
Patricia Ann
Patricia Ann
Patricia Barbara
Patricia Bernice
Patricia Daisy
Patricia Dawn
Patricia Elizabeth
Patricia Lesley
Patricia Wendy
Patsy Ann
Patti
Paula Diane

Pauline Teresa
Penelope Eve
Penelope Jane
Penny Sue
Petra
Petrina Rose
Peyton Lois
Philippa Catherine
Phoebe
Phoebe Adele
Phoebe Grace
Phoebe Lynn
Phoebe Sam
Phoenix Melodie
Phyllis Joanne
Pippa
Pippa Jane
Pixie Isabel
Polly Ann
Polly Hermione
Polly Sarah
Poppy
Poppy 90
Poppy Elizabeth
Poppy Ella
Poppy Isla
Poppy Kate
Poppy Rose
Poppy Ruth
Primrose
Queenie Beth
Quinn Mae
Rachael Elizabeth
Rachael Thora
Rachel
Rachel Ann
Rachel Dawn
Rachel Emma
Rachel Jane
Rachel Kath
Rachel Leanne
Rachel Lynn
Rachel Maia
Rachel Michelle
Rachel Miranda
Raia Elise

Rebecca
Rebecca
Rebecca
Rebecca Alice
Rebecca Ann
Rebecca Emily
Rebecca Emily Hannah
Rebecca Francis
Rebecca Hazel
Rebecca Jane
Rebecca Megan
Rebecca Naomi
Rebecca Rachel
Rebecca Renee
Rebecca Teresa
Rebecca Tracey
Reeya Dana
Renata Paulina
Rhian Hannah
Rhianna Amber
Rhianna Jayne
Rhiannon Kimberley
Rhoda Patricia
Rhonda Patricia
Riley Celyn
Rita
Rita Sian
Robyn Elizabeth
Rochelle Patricia
Rosa Eleanor
Rosalyn Julia
Rosanagh Catherine
Rosanna Joan
Rosanna May
Rose
Rose Eleanor
Rose Gwyneth
Rose Thewlis
Roseada
Rosella May
Rosemary Florence
Rosemary Lynne
Rosie Jane
Rosie Jayne
Rosie Louise
Rosie Mae

Rosina Jean
Rovina Bridget
Rowan
Rowena Mary
Ruby Emma
Ruby Grace
Ruby Jo
Ruby Lola
Ruby Louise
Ruby Mae
Ruby May
Ruby Rose
Ruth
Ruth
Ruth Ina
Ruth Lauren
Ruth Louise
Sabina
Sadie Joy
Sadie Nicola
Saffiyah Malika
Sally Alice
Sally Bess
Sally Caroline
Sally Lesley
Sally Victoria
Sam
Sam Elissa
Samantha Abbey
Samantha Erja
Samantha Jane
Samantha Jane
Samantha Jayne
Samantha Jayne
Samantha Joanne
Samantha Kaye
Samantha Rose
Samantha Tiegan
Sammi Jo
Sammy Liz
Samoana Louise
Sandie Jayne
Sandra Elizabeth
Sandra Jayne
Sandra Lesley
Sandra Rosalyn

Sandra Wilma
Sandy Sam
Sanita Moya
Sara Clare
Sara Lee
Sarah
Sarah Elizabeth
Sarah Gabriella
Sarah Hannah
Sarah Louise
Sarah Marie
Sarah Pamela
Sarannah Kate
Sascha Angel
Sasha Louise
Sasha Louise
Savannah Rose
Scarlett
Scarlett Rose
Seane Leigh
Selina Mia
Serafina
Serena Joan
Shani Patrena
Shania Agnes
Shannon Chloe
Shannon Denise
Shannon Meghann
Shannon Rose
Sharman Agnes
Sharon
Sharon Jayne
Sharon Lesley
Sharon Lisa
Sharon Miriam
Sheena Elise
Sheena Margaret
Sheila Ann
Sheila Anne
Sheila Katie
Sheila Leslie
Sheila Mary
Shelbi Evangaline
Shelbie Marie
Shelby Ann
Shelby Jenna

Shelia Anne
Shelly Louise
Sheridan Marie
Sheridan Michelle
Shiela Margaret
Shirlee June
Shirley Margaret
Shirley Naomi
Shona
Sienna Belle
Sienna Belle
Simone
Sinead Eimear
Siobhan Christie
Siona Rose
Sky Rebecca
Skye Heather
Skye Mae
Skye Maisie
Sommer May
Sonia Patricia
Sonia Rachel
Sonya Dawn
Sophia Rose
Sophie
Sophie Alex
Sophie Caroline
Sophie Catherine
Sophie Elise
Sophie Elizabeth
Sophie Ellena
Sophie Grace
Sophie Jane
Sophie Jessica
Sophie Jessica
Sophie Johanna
Sophie Lauren
Sophie Louise
Sophie Lucy
Sophie Rose
Sqn Ldr Sue
Stacey
Stacey Joanne
Stacey Joanne
Staci
Stephanie Alice

Stephanie Elizabeth
Stephanie Kate
Stephanie Michelle
Stephanie Susanne
Stephanie Victoria
Stephanie Violet
Stephannie June
Stevie Kim
Sue Carly
Sue Rose
Summer Charlotte
Summer Patience
Susahnellah
Susan
Susan Barbara
Susan Betty
Susan Carole
Susan Dallas
Susan Edith
Susan Jane
Susan Margaret
Susannah Margaret
Suzanne Jane
Suzanne Lesley
Suzanne Louise
Suzanne Patricia
Suzanne Patricia
Suzette Elizabeth
Suzie Olivia
Suzy B
Sydney Cadence
Sylverine
Sylvia Diane
Talia Brooke
Tammi Leanne
Tammy Olivia
Tamsin Helen
Tamsyn Susan
Tanya Louise
Tanya Marie
Tara Trudy
Tarryn Leigh
Tassie
Taya Jayne
Taya Mai
Taylor Freya

Taylor Paige
Taz
Tegan Ami
Tegwen Anne
Tellytubby
Teresa Lorraine
Teresa Marie
Terri Ann
Thalia Amber
Thalia Rose
Thelma Mary
Thirza Helen
Thomke Tania
Tia Rose
Tiana Lousie
Tiarna
Tillie Violet
Tilly Gio
Tilly Rose
Tina
Toni Karen
Toni Rebecca
Tonia
Torby
Toyka
Tracey Adele
Tracey Cerise
Tracey Diane
Tracey Holly
Tracy
Tracy
Tracy
Tracy Dorothy
Tracy Jacqi
Tracy Kerry
Tricia Kelly
Trina Inathe
Trinity Cassandra
Trinity Rj
Trish
Trudie
Trudy
Trylena Jane
Tyomee
Tyra Dion
Valentino

Valerie Lee
Vanessa Bethany
Vera
Vera Carolyn
Verity Jean
Verity Lauren
Veronica Lilly
Vicky Lyn
Victoire Terena
Victoria Elaine
Victoria Isobel
Victoria Jane
Victoria Julie
Vikki Louise
Violet Jean
Violet Josephine
Violet Louise
Vivien Margaret
Vivienne Esther
Wanda
Wendy Elizabeth
Wendy Jane
Wendy Joy
Wendy Margaret
Wendy Michelle
Wendy Teresa
Whitney Michelle
Willow
Wilma Joan
Yvonne
Yvonne Diane
Yvonne Louisa
Zahra Lydia
Zahra Michelle
Zara
Zara Emily
Zara Isla
Zara Jade
Zephine Bridget
Zoe Denise
Zoe Frances
Zoe Jane
Zoe Jane
Zoe Stephanie
Zoe Victoria

RECOMMENDED READING

The Eddie Stobart Story by Hunter Davies
(Harper Collins)
Only The Best Will Do: The Eddie Stobart Story
by Eddie and Nora Stobart with Noel Davidson
(Ambassador Books).

ACKNOWLEDGEMENTS

I would particularly like to thank Laura Tinkler for her
exceptional assistance in helping me collate all the
interviews necessary for this book. Special thanks also
to William Stobart and Andrew Tinkler for their time
and support.

This book would have been much less fun without
the energetic help of Mark Dixon, Tim Fox, Fiona
Soltysiak, Lee Humphreys, Andrew Whiles, Rachel
Invinson Simpson, Bonnie Stephenson, Andrew Kidd and
Lorna-Dawn Creanor.

Special thanks to my publisher Lorna Russell
and editor Hannah Knowles for making this such an
enjoyable project to work on. Heads up also to Henry
Russell and Ian Gittins.

A special thank you also to Princess Productions
for their amazing TV series, *Eddie Stobart: Trucks
and Trailers*. These hugely popular programmes were
essential research for the writing of this book and the
author would like to duly acknowledge the programme
makers' expertise here.

Virgin Books would like to thank Simon and David
Mulholland for all their help with providing the pictures
for this book.

EDDIE STOBART – TRUCKS & TRAILERS

Launched in September 2010, three successful series of
Trucks & Trailers have now aired on Channel 5. The total
reach across all episodes of *Trucks & Trailers* (including
repeats) is an impressive 24.2 million viewers. As well as
being superb secondary research for the author, these
shows are essential viewing for any Eddie fanatic; what
struck me during the writing of this book was the huge
detail the production company went into even when
capturing the smallest sequence.

10 9 8 7 6 5 4 3 2

First published in the United Kingdom in 2012 by Virgin Books,
an imprint of Ebury Publishing

A Random House Group Company

Copyright © Stobart Group Ltd and Martin Roach 2012

Stobart Group Ltd and Martin Roach have asserted their right
under the Copyright, Designs and Patents Act 1988 to be
identified as the authors of this work.

Pictures supplied by Mulholland Media

Every reasonable effort has been made to contact copyright
holders of material reproduced in this book. If any have
inadvertently been overlooked, the publishers would be glad to
hear from them and make good in future editions any errors or
omissions brought to their attention.

Addresses for companies within The Random House Group
Limited can be found at www.randomhouse.co.uk/offices.htm

The Random House Group Limited Reg. No. 954009

A CIP catalogue record for this book is available from the
British Library

The Random House Group Limited supports The Forest
Stewardship Council (FSC®), the leading international forest
certification organisation. Our books carrying the FSC label
are printed on FSC® certified paper. FSC is the only forest
certification scheme endorsed by the leading environmental
organisations, including Greenpeace.
Our paper procurement policy can be found at www.
randomhouse.co.uk/environment

FSC — MIX — Paper from responsible sources — FSC® C016897 — www.fsc.org

Printed and bound in the United Kingdom by Butler, Tanner &
Dennis Ltd.

ISBN: 9780753540909

To buy books by your favourite authors and register for offers,
visit www.randomhouse.co.uk